36 WORKSHOPS TO GET KIDS WRITING

ALA Editions purchases fund advocacy, awareness, and accreditation programs for library professionals worldwide.

36 WORKSHOPS TO GET KIDS WRITING
FROM ALIENS TO ZEBRAS

ANNMARIE HURTADO

ALA Editions

CHICAGO | 2018

ANNMARIE HURTADO has worked in schools and libraries for more than eight years and for five years has been a librarian in the Youth Services Department of the Pasadena (California) Public Library. There she created a bilingual yearlong reading program called Lucha Libros for elementary school students and facilitated a mother–daughter book club, a series of hands-on science workshops, and two monthly creative writing workshops, each tailored to different age groups—one is for tweens 9 to 12 years old, and the other is for kids 5 to 8 years old who are still developing their basic writing skills. It is Hurtado's experience with the latter group that inspired her to write this book.

. . . .

© 2018 by the American Library Association

Extensive effort has gone into ensuring the reliability of the information in this book; however, the publisher makes no warranty, express or implied, with respect to the material contained herein.

ISBN: 978-0-8389-1648-3 (paper)

Names: Hurtado, AnnMarie, author.
Title: 36 workshops to get kids writing : from aliens to zebras / AnnMarie Hurtado.
Description: Chicago : ALA Editions, an imprint of the American Library Association, 2018. | Includes
    bibliographical references and index.
Identifiers: LCCN 2017031633 | ISBN 9780838916483 (pbk. : alk. paper)
Subjects: LCSH: Children's libraries—Activity programs—United States. | School libraries—Activity
    programs—United States. | Creative writing (Primary education)—United States. | English language—
    Composition and exercises—Study and teaching (Primary)—United States.
Classification: LCC Z718.3 .H87 2018 | DDC 027.62/5--dc23 LC record available at https://lccn.loc.gov/
2017031633

Cover design by Krista Joy Johnson. Book design by Alejandra Diaz in the Chaparral Pro, Gotham and GoodGirl typefaces.

♾ This paper meets the requirements of ANSI/NISO Z39.48–1992 (Permanence of Paper).

Printed in the United States of America
22 21 20 19 18   5 4 3 2 1

For Sali, who already is a writer

CONTENTS

ACKNOWLEDGMENTS

First and foremost, a huge thanks to my editor, Jamie Santoro, for everything she did to bring this book to fruition. Without her support this book would never have become a reality! From the very beginning she gave me the benefit of her keen insight and uplifting encouragement. I am so lucky I got to work with such a wonderful person. I am deeply grateful to Angela Gwizdala for taking this book to final publication and to Carolyn Crabtree for being an excellent copy editor. Thanks for making this a better book!

Thank you to the designers for taking my sometimes complicated, weird handout ideas and making them into beautiful, fun canvases for children to create with!

Thanks to my parents—Joyce, a primary school educator with over thirty years of teaching experience, and Larry, a musician and artist. They raised me to love the arts and to believe in myself as a writer from a very early age.

Thanks to my sisters, Amanda and Monica—I've thought of you often while writing this book about creative writing experiences for kids because you taught me how to write in that backyard where we played and acted out our stories every day.

I'm grateful to the school librarian from my elementary school, Michelle Macnamara, for being one of the first people to encourage me to be a writer. She passed away in 2017, and I wish she knew how fondly I thought of her.

Thanks to all my teachers from grade school and high school who read my early writing out loud and treated it like it was worth something. And I'd like to give a shout-out to my daughter's first-grade teacher, Kimberly Enriquez, who reminded her every day that she is *already* a writer.

Thanks to everyone at Pasadena Public Library, the incredibly talented and supportive colleagues who I've been blessed to work with for five years.

Writing in the Library
A Radical Idea

I magine you are asking a child what a person can do in a library. "Read books," you will hear—after all, we already know that, in the eyes of our public, books are our brand.[1] What else can you do in the library? Depending on the child's experience, you might hear other answers: "Go to storytime." "Do arts and crafts." "Join a book club." "Play with puzzles." "Go to a magic show." "Hear a band play." "Do a science experiment." "Claim a prize in Summer Reading." What do all these answers have in common? Not necessarily books. For many decades now, *literacy,* not books, has been the true emphasis of most children's services in the library. And most children's librarians can tell you that books alone are not the sole foundation of literacy. Early literacy is all about talking, singing, playing, reading, and writing.[2] We figure we've got most of these covered in our library's storytimes, music shows, art programs, book clubs, and play areas.

Talking, singing, playing, reading, and . . . writing.

Where's the writing?

And a more urgent question: Where's the writing for the kids who need it the most, as they are learning *how* to read and write?

Most language arts teachers are familiar with the research going back decades showing that children *learn to read through writing.* But librarians have missed out on that literature. We tell ourselves that we are about encouraging children to read. We tell parents over and over that children learn to read when you read to them great books that appeal to them—and that is true! But we don't think about how children learn to write when you let them write for fun, and that writing is a vital and necessary part of building a child's *reading* skills.

So once again, where's the writing?

"All across the country, libraries are offering writing programs for adults and teens," writes Ally Blumenfeld in a 2016 blog post on the *Library as Incubator Project* website.[3] But do a search for public libraries offering writing programs for children in the primary grades, and chances are good you won't find many. Librarians might be forgiven for thinking that offering creative writing workshops to children in kindergarten is a radical idea—even as those same librarians put on frequent art programs, craft programs, science programs, and music. How is it that our profession has come so far in offering creative writing opportunities to young adults while ignoring the needs of the youngest and earliest writers who are at the critical age where they are developing an identity grounded in literacy?

Our emphasis on promoting reading greatly outweighs any efforts we make to do programming about the other side of literacy—writing. Consider the prevalence of summer reading programs across the United States and other countries around the world, and then try to find a single public library advertising writing workshops for children under the age of 8.

Have libraries been failing to emphasize the importance of *writing* in their efforts to push more reading? Nearly thirty years ago, James Moffett criticized the nation's schools for favoring reading over writing, making both "harder to master," while simultaneously making students "more the consumers of others' thinking than original thinkers themselves."[4] Kay Cowan wrote in 2001 that "the emphasis on writing in our classrooms and in the research literature is minimal compared to the attention given reading."[5] A decade and a half later, educators and researchers are *still* talking about the "apparent dominance of reading over writing in schools."[6]

Do these same complaints apply to libraries? Despite our devotion to books, is there more we could be doing to promote *literacy?* And what can librarians do to promote creative writing, not just for teens but for primary-grade students as well?

CHILDREN LEARN TO READ BY WRITING

This tendency to support only the reading side of literacy when serving children in primary grades ignores more than thirty years of education research which tells us that reading and writing develop simultaneously in *early* childhood. "Just as they figure out the complex phonology, grammar, and vocabulary of spoken English by about the age of five," write Jean Wallace Gillet and Lynn Beverly, "children figure out much of what writing is and how it works entirely by experiences with it, in about the same time frame."[7]

Just as children learn to read by being read to, and in their early attempts at reading they show that they notice the correspondence of print with the sounds they hear, children learn how words are formed by early attempts at writing. This process starts with their earliest scribbles, which, according to the toddler, stand for words. As they learn the alphabet and develop invented spellings, indicating their growing understanding of which letters to assign to a particular word or sound, they are developing important strategies that they need to read words.[8]

Over the years, primary-grade teachers have emphasized a reciprocal, "two-for-one" kind of relationship between reading and writing, which helps students acquire both skills more quickly.[9] Ruth Culham calls the two skills of reading and writing a "one-two punch": "When we work on the skills related to one, we quite naturally work on the other."[10]

When children do *creative* writing, they bring all that developing print awareness and early literacy together with play and imagination to push themselves to express their ideas. It is so important for children in kindergarten through first grade to have creative writing opportunities, because creative writing is a *child-driven* activity that motivates them to learn how to write and makes them better readers. As the child is deciding which words to use and comes across a word he does not know how to spell, the child sounds out the word and attempts to write it down anyway. The child is driven internally to increase his literacy, word by word, when writing something that comes from the imagination in a fun, friendly learning environment.

WRITING IS PLAY

A 1999 study by researchers Danling Fu and Jane Townsend followed seven children through two years from kindergarten to first grade to determine how different teachers' approaches to teaching writing might impact the children's academic growth and literacy skills. What the researchers found was astonishing (and downright heartbreaking). The same children who flourished at or above grade level with a kindergarten teacher who encouraged daily creative writing became stifled and miserable about writing with a first-grade teacher who treated creative writing as an exercise in correct punctuation and spelling.

First let's look at how the kindergarten teacher's emphasis on reading and creative writing activities every day promoted the children's overall academic performance:

> By the end of the year, the seven children selected as our case studies all passed the grade requirement test; two of them were above grade level (Eddie was one of these), and the rest were at grade level. The test evaluated three areas: letter naming, phonemic awareness, and book concepts. This class, which did more writing than did any of the other four kindergarten classes at the school, received the highest average grade-level score. When asked how she accounted for the high score, the teacher said that she thought the children's frequent writing activities had made the difference.[11]

Now contrast this picture of children writing joyfully and scoring high academically with the following picture of those same children just a few months later, when they were asked to undertake endless, meaningless writing worksheets intended for little other than testing the children's knowledge of writing conventions:

> Eddie . . . proved himself to be a writer in kindergarten. But the worksheet writing [in first grade] didn't give him any chance or room to be creative, to think and imagine, or even to experiment with language. He learned to put forth the least effort and get the best grade, to write nonsense, to use words without much meaning. He also learned that school reading and writing were not for personal expression or communication. Keith, a boy in the same class, said it all when asked if he understood what he was doing. "No," he said, "I just do it."
>
> What does writing mean to Eddie? When asked in an interview at the end of his first-grade year how he might improve himself as a writer, Eddie responded: "To write with the best handwriting, the straightest writing like the computer does." His words tell us that he had learned that "good" writing has little to do with creativity or with providing information. Eddie's first-grade view differs sharply from what he said at the end of kindergarten when what he valued in his writing were the "good words" and "good stories."[12]

The story of young Eddie is a cautionary tale for anyone teaching children to read and write, because even as it demonstrates the academic achievement possible by providing children more opportunities for creative writing, it unfortunately details the tragic destruction of their enthusiasm for learning after their new teacher's methods sucked all the creativity out of the process. Certainly it is important for children to learn the conventions of print, spelling, grammar, and sentence structure. But this learning will happen in time, the more they write. As teachers and librarians, we must find a way to set aside time for children to write simply for the *joy* of it, with no expectations or demands attached. Otherwise, children will come to resist writing and avoid it at all costs. In the words of Lucy McCormick Calkins, "We forget that we, too, would yawn and roll our eyes if we were asked to write about our summer vacation or our favorite food. We do not consider how we would feel if the only response to our hard-earned stories were red-penned 'Awks' and 'Run-ons.'"[13] There is a place for instruction in grammar and print conventions, but first children need to be given a safe space for exploring and dreaming, and that is what I suggest a library writing program or primary-grade classroom workshop can be.

CHILDREN WRITE *BEFORE* THEY CAN SPELL

It is putting the cart before the horse to expect children to learn how to spell before being invited to write anything fun or meaningful. Sara Ackerman said it quite well: "[C]hildren are not expected to refrain from speaking until they have fully grasped oral language. Likewise, they should not be expected to form letters neatly, spell perfectly, or use punctuation accurately before being invited to write."[14] Between the ages of 3 and 5, children are discovering that "marks on paper have the power to make meaning."[15] It is not important yet to make sure that those marks can be published in an academic journal. Rather, at this early age, it is simply necessary that we as educators and librarians "respond" in a positive way: "Just as infants learn the power of their gestures through our response to those gestures, language learners discover the power of their print and pictures through our response."[16] While young children play with telling stories by putting marks on paper, and eventually make those marks with letters, it is up to us to support those children and applaud their progress.

Even as children get old enough to learn to spell, there will be misspellings, and these errors are an important sign of learning. "Spelling progress is shown not necessarily by fewer errors, but by errors that show more complex strategies."[17] These errors are actually "signs of intelligent, ambitious language use rather than deficiency."[18]

Dare to challenge the idea that making spelling errors is a "bad" thing, and, instead, find the growth and motivation contained in them. Let us encourage young children to write, and to write *boldly!*

WRITING IS NOT TOO ACADEMIC, IF DONE RIGHT

In recent years, many educators and parents have expressed concerns that kindergarten is becoming too academic—"the new first grade"—and is not giving children enough opportunities for play. These concerns are valid. But please do not assume that these concerns apply to the act of *creative* writing. Creative writing *is* play. Calkins said it best: "It is not children—but adults—who have separated writing from art, song, and play; it is adults who have turned writing into an exercise on dotted-line paper, into a matter of rules, lessons, and cautious behavior."[19] When done well, creative writing lessons for kindergartners can offer plenty of opportunities for silliness and imagination, especially when we weave in singing, talking, reading, playing—in other words, when we give writing the support of the other four early literacy practices that can bolster it and help it thrive.

Deborah Wells Rowe, Joanne Deal Fitch, and Alyson Smith Bass had great success when giving children toys during writing workshops and encouraging the children to use the toys to make up stories and then write down those stories. The authors followed the children's natural inclination to play pretend and helped the children talk out those stories and transcribe them. It just takes a little time for the magic to work. "We found that children often developed their most creative ideas after 20–30 minutes of play. It often took this much time for children to select characters, negotiate their roles and relationships, develop some agreement on the nature of the story world, and explore plot ideas."[20]

Others have found that simply introducing conversation and collaboration can turn the whole process into one of *play*. Kay Cowan used a tape recorder to record the stories her students came up with orally and then gave them support with writing down the stories. Cowan also noted that some students consistently preferred to begin with drawings and then used drawing as their vehicle for working out their ideas.[21] Finally, acting out stories has been another important avenue used by teachers to help children start creating written stories. "Once children were comfortable with generating stories by playing with toys and other objects, they often suggested acting out stories written by others as a way of understanding and enjoying them."[22]

The research showing how kindergartners respond to creative writing activities has been consistently positive. There is truly no scientific basis for assuming that teaching creative writing to 5-year-olds is expecting too much or placing too heavy a burden on the children. Quite the contrary—it opens them up to new possibilities and is usually embraced enthusiastically by the kids. When Maria Berzins started encouraging her kindergarten students to write from their very first day in school in 1998, her 5-year-old students became "consumed with a kind of literacy fever—they wanted to read and write all the time! Expecting students to write from the first day of kindergarten allowed their potential for literacy to unfold much earlier and helped motivate and encourage them as emergent writers."[23] What Berzins learned was an echo of what kindergarten teachers before her had begun trying ever since Lucy Calkins wrote in 1986: "[C]hildren can write sooner than we ever dreamed was possible."[24]

HUMOR IS AN ESSENTIAL PART OF PLAY

Humor is one of the primary connections that children make between books and play. We see it as they return again and again to their favorite funny books, and we see it develop as they share their early attempts at humor. There is something about humor writing that not only is entertaining for both the writer and the audience but also stretches children's imaginations and motivates young writers to revise their work in a quest for more fun.[25] Humor can also create a kind of "even playing field" between children and grownups because we can all connect over a funny story and admit to times when we are being foolish or silly.

For that reason, when we get into the writing lessons based on picture books, you will notice that I place a very heavy emphasis on funny picture books. When children are laughing, they are emboldened to make more courageous and outgoing choices in their writing. They take more risks. And when children are feeling shy, unsure of what to write or where to begin, laughter can be a very effective icebreaker.

BUT I'M NOT A TEACHER, JUST A LIBRARIAN

I hope you're laughing as you read that, because no one is "just" a librarian. Most libraries serving children already provide programs teaching crafts, inviting them to draw or paint, build with LEGOs, do hands-on science activities, learn computing skills, and more. And although the role of the youth services librarian or school librarian may not be the same as that of a teacher, getting familiar with some of the research on literacy development that has informed generations of primary-grade teachers can have enormous benefits for the work of youth services librarians to encourage and promote literacy. The National Council of Teachers of English (NCTE) crystallizes some of that research in its official position on the teaching of writing, saying that writing helps children "become better readers": "In their earliest writing experiences, children listen for the relationships of sounds to letters, which contributes greatly to their phonemic awareness and phonics knowledge."[26] The NCTE's position statement is written for teachers, but there are lots of ways that librarians can take it to heart and help teachers with that mission. Consider the following skills that the NCTE recommends for teachers:

> In order to provide high-quality writing opportunities for all students, teachers need to understand:
>
> - How writers read for the purposes of writing—with an eye toward not just what the text says but also how it is put together;
> - The psychological and social processes reading and writing have in common;
> - The ways writers imagine their intended readers, anticipating their responses and needs;
> - That text structures are fluid enough to accommodate frequent exceptions, innovations, and disruptions;
> - How writers can identify mentor or exemplar texts, both print and digital, that they may want to emulate in their own writing.[27]

Librarians can help by being aware of "mentor or exemplar texts," and we can make sure to carry those texts in our collections to support primary-grade teachers and young writers. We can help also by providing more opportunities for creative writing in our programming. Although we cannot replace the role of the teacher, we can provide a great deal of extra enrichment and support to both teacher and child.

In its "Position Statement on the School Librarian's Role in Reading," the American Association of School Librarians encourages school librarians to take this kind of role:

> - School librarians take a leadership role in organizing and promoting literacy projects and events that engage learners and motivate them to become lifelong readers.

- Classroom teachers, reading specialists, and school librarians select materials, promote the curricular and independent use of resources, including traditional and alternative materials, and plan learning experiences that offer whole classes, small groups, and individual learners an interdisciplinary approach to literacy learning.[28]

The activities in this book will help you create those interdisciplinary learning experiences. When students come to your library to be introduced to a hilarious book and do a fun writing activity, they will associate the library with literacy on a whole new level in which they are more than just consumers of the books in your collection.

CREATIVE WRITING AND THE COMMON CORE

People have many opinions about the Common Core State Standards, but one thing is undeniable: the new standards "take a clear stand on behalf of reading and writing across the curriculum."[29] According to Ruth Culham, "Writing has finally taken a place at the big family table with reading and math,"[30] and it's true—writing has infiltrated and permeated *all* the academic subjects, as it always should have. In the past, test-taking skills, solving problems in the conventional way, and selecting the right answer were considered paramount to success in mathematics. Now, you'll notice that the ability to write a few sentences about the process for solving the problem is a staple feature of math homework.

There is also a more holistic approach to literacy in the Common Core, which I believe teachers and librarians will find welcome. As Rachel Wadham and Terrell Young wrote, "Ultimately the Core defines literacy as more than reading and writing, as it also puts an emphasis on communication, collaboration, creativity, problem solving, technology, citizenship, information literacy, and life skills."[31] And creative writing, in particular, offers countless opportunities for exploring those skills.

COMMON CORE STANDARDS IN THE PRIMARY GRADES

As you go through the activities in this book, you will see frequent references to specific Common Core Standards, listed in detail at the beginning of each chapter and referenced at the beginning of each lesson. The standards themselves change only a little from one grade level to the next, adding a bit more each year, so I have defaulted to the ones for second grade. But it will be useful to start your work with this book by reviewing those differences.

Let's take a look at the first few writing standards for kindergarten and explore how they change as children progress into first and second grade.

CCSS.ELA-LITERACY.W.K.1: Use a combination of drawing, dictating, and writing to compose opinion pieces in which they tell a reader the topic or the name of the book they are writing about and state an opinion or preference about the topic or book (e.g., *My favorite book is . . .*).

CCSS.ELA-LITERACY.W.K.2: Use a combination of drawing, dictating, and writing to compose informative/explanatory texts in which they name what they are writing about and supply some information about the topic.

CCSS.ELA-LITERACY.W.K.3: Use a combination of drawing, dictating, and writing to narrate a single event or several loosely linked events, tell about the events in the order in which they occurred, and provide a reaction to what happened.

By first grade, children's writing should have developed to the point at which their opinion pieces "supply a reason for the opinion, and provide a sense of closure," their informational texts provide more "facts," and their narratives include more "details" (italics added):

CCSS.ELA-LITERACY.W.1.1: Write opinion pieces in which they introduce the topic or name the book they are writing about, state an opinion, *supply a reason for the opinion, and provide some sense of closure.*

CCSS.ELA-LITERACY.W.1.2: Write informative/explanatory texts in which they name a topic, *supply some facts about the topic, and provide some sense of closure.*

CCSS.ELA-LITERACY.W.1.3: Write narratives in which they recount two or more appropriately sequenced events, include some *details* regarding what happened, *use temporal words to signal event order, and provide some sense of closure.*

By second grade, children should be using more "linking words to connect opinions and reasons" and learning about transitions. They should also be using "temporal words" to signify the order of events in their narrative writing and be putting more emphasis on "actions, thoughts, and feelings" (italics added):

CCSS.ELA-LITERACY.W.2.1: Write opinion pieces in which they introduce the topic or book they are writing about, state an opinion, supply reasons that support the opinion, *use linking words* (e.g., because, and, also*) to connect opinion and reasons, and provide a concluding statement or section.*

CCSS.ELA-LITERACY.W.2.2: Write informative/explanatory texts in which they introduce a topic, *use facts and definitions to develop points,* and provide a concluding statement or section.

CCSS.ELA-LITERACY.W.2.3: Write narratives in which they recount a well-elaborated event or short sequence of events, *include details to describe actions, thoughts, and feelings,* use temporal words to signal event order, and provide a sense of closure.

It's not that kindergartners or first graders cannot supply details about their thoughts or feelings, or use facts or linking words in their writing. The standards merely imply that by the time they finish second grade, all students should be capable of that level of complexity. The standards are a benchmark, but I have met kindergartners who were capable of meeting that benchmark much earlier than the standards would require.

You will note that, throughout this book, I refer to additional Common Core Standards that are not included in the "Writing" section but have been assigned to the "Reading" or "Language" sections of the standards. Personally, I agree with Susan Martin and Sherry Dismuke's argument that this categorizing creates an "artificial separation" of the foundational skills for reading from other skills needed for writing.[32] Especially where early writers are concerned, the ability to "generalize learned spelling patterns when writing words" (**CCSS.ELA -LITERACY.L.2.2.D**) or to "identify real-life connections between words and their use (e.g., *describe foods that are spicy or juicy*)" (**CCSS.ELA-LITERACY.L.2.5.A**) is, of course, relevant to the act of writing anything. So wherever possible, I have attempted to bring together *all* the English language arts standards that would apply to each lesson in this book.

My other complaint about the Common Core State Standards for writing is that the recommended literary forms are sometimes too narrow. Poetry, letter writing, journal writing, and other formats don't always fall neatly into the categories of "narrative writing, informational writing, and opinion/argumentative writing." Nonetheless, I will show how each activity in this book, regardless of its genre or format, involves the skills children need to achieve proficiency in those required types of writing. I just hope that, as the standards are refined and expanded in years to come, they will include a more diverse variety of writing genres just as they have successfully pervaded a diverse variety of school subjects. Writing activities such as comic strips, funny stories, circus posters, and riddles can all support the development of a strong foundation in writing arguments and organizing ideas as well as promote the "command of sequence and detail that are essential for effective argumentative and informative writing."[33]

USING THESE LESSONS IN THE CLASSROOM

The thirty-six lesson plans provided in this book are intended as a weekly supplement to the daily practice of doing writing workshop. I am referring to the concept taught by Lucy Calkins in her 1986 book *The Art of Teaching Writing*, which urges teachers "to set aside an hour a day, every day, for the writing workshop" while warning that "[i]t is almost impossible to create an effective writing workshop if students write only once or twice a week."[34] Encouraging your students to sit down and write about whatever comes into their heads, and to work on revising drafts they have already written, should be a daily routine in every classroom. But sometimes children need a prompt, a new starting point for generating ideas. That is why I suggest making these activities a once-a-week or once-a-month practice, to spice things up and to give your kids new prompts and expose them to new mentor texts.

PRESENTING THESE PROGRAMS IN THE LIBRARY

Unlike teachers, librarians don't often get to follow each child's progress over the course of a year or have the benefit of seeing a child's project morph from draft to draft. Most school librarians get to see each child only once a week, and the frequency is much less for public librarians. With that in mind, these writing workshops were developed to work like any other stand-alone children's craft or art program that you might do at a public or school library, with the output being a work of creative writing inspired by a popular children's book.

To me, it was always important that my library writing workshops—I call them "Writing Parties"—draw explicit inspiration from the books in my library's collection. I try to lead the kids to engage with the books as a writer would, and I find that they are usually eager and capable of developing a deeper understanding of the author's craft. Roy Corden studied this approach more formally and found that when quality children's literature is used, children develop a "metalanguage" that they readily apply to discussing their own writing—even primary-grade children can absorb such concepts as literary devices and can talk about a text's effectiveness, once they see someone break down those concepts using concrete examples from books they enjoy.[35]

When you read kids a book that prompts a creative or wacky suggestion, such as "What would happen if someone tried to organize a panda parade?" or "What would a scary public service announcement about evil butterflies actually look like?," kids jump at the challenge of creating that concept and bringing it into existence, engaging with the book on a new level. I discovered this outcome for myself when I read the book *A Pig Parade Is a Terrible Idea* by Michael Ian Black and Kevin Hawkes to my daughter (who was 5 at the time). She loved how the book ended with the suggestion that a panda parade might work out better. She said, "That was so funny! Can you bring home *Panda Parade* tomorrow?"

I said, "I don't think they've written that book. But *you* could write it." My daughter was more interested in puppies and kittens than pandas, so she wrote a picture book called *A Puppie Parade Is a Terrible Idea* (her spelling). This response inspired me to find out whether other picture books could provide creative writing ideas for kindergartners like my daughter, which led me to develop these programs and write this book.

Librarians, picture this with me: once a week or once a month, children between the ages of 5 and 8 are invited to a fun event at the library in a festive, decorative environment. They will hear a funny story told by an expert storyteller (you) and then they will be encouraged to find some inspiration in that story to create their own book (or poem or another kind of creative writing).

When they are finished, they will participate in a different kind of "storytime" in which *they* will be the storytellers. With the handouts and book templates we've created, most of these programs will take only a few minutes to prepare, though the parents will think you spent hours on them. The children will come away remembering the fun activities they did at the library, proud of the stories they created there.

ENGLISH LANGUAGE LEARNERS

Whether you work in a school setting or a public one, you're going to encounter children with a wide range of prior experience with writing, with telling stories, and with communicating in English. This book will give you ideas to help English language learners and give them extra scaffolding, so that they can benefit from these creative writing programs.

I have seen English language learners grow by leaps and bounds when their imaginations are set free in a low-pressure, high-literacy environment. When I first started doing these writing workshops at the library, there was a Korean family whose boys (ages 5 and 7) always attended but who struggled to write for a long time because they were still learning English. The boys had limited conversational skills (and I don't speak Korean), but I would often sit with them and talk about story ideas or ask them about the pictures they were drawing, trying to elicit more information about what interested them. They liked humor. They would ask me to write things for them or spell words, and I would help them, but I always got the sense that they felt lost. After six months, however, I noticed a change when the 7-year-old wrote (independently) a story about a fly who flew away from home because his mom always made him eat his vegetables. Both boys were laughing and excited, and I was just overjoyed for them! I couldn't take all the credit for this transformation and felt sure that they must have had very good classroom teachers, but I do think that coming to these creative writing programs helped them, over time, absorb a lot of new language, come out of their shells, and start engaging in English writing for fun.

Often, the standard environment in which English language learners are placed is very restrictive, with a reductionist approach to learning to write. Nadeen Ruiz, Eleanor Vargas, and Angelica Beltran wrote of this reductionist approach:

> Characteristics of reductionist instruction include an overwhelming focus on fragments of texts such as letters and single words (in the hopes that conquering the subskills of literacy will add up to proficient reading and writing); on copying (in the hopes that inculcating "good habits" such as correct spelling will prevent "bad habits" such as incorrect spelling); and on comprehending specially constructed texts with little reference to students' experiences (in the hopes that practicing with phonetically or lexically controlled texts will lead to comprehension of authentic

texts). Studies show that these hopes were not realized: bilingual students achieved poorly or showed limited engagement in reductionist instructional contexts.[36]

If those Korean children were confined, like so many other kids, to a reductionist classroom for English language learners, how likely would it be that they would have found themselves writing a funny story about a frustrated, rebellious fly? Would they be reading texts that were appropriate for their age and interests and developing sense of humor, or babyish texts chosen specifically to advance a limited development in English vocabulary and decoding skills?

Instead, at the library they found a program that promoted deep engagement with texts full of silly, exciting ideas, and an environment that said, "Write a book of your own—the sky's the limit!" I can't help but think that encouragement was important in their growth. I think Ruiz, Vargas, and Beltran would agree, too, because they wrote that a major principle of effective instruction with English language learners involves creating "opportunities for students to meaningfully and authentically apply their developing oral language and literacy skills."[37] These authors recommend encouraging English language learners to study authentic children's literature, not just texts that have been chosen for promoting phonics or decoding skills, because such reading "ups the ante for active participation when compared to other types of reading instruction."[38] The more often English language learners are encouraged to talk about books, make notes and lists, brainstorm ideas, and talk about story ideas they are still developing, the more likely they are to be able to produce creative writing that is internally motivated and authentic.

Researchers have recommended several strategies that have demonstrably helped English language learners learn to write: interactive journals (in which both teacher and student converse in writing, and the teacher writes comments about the student's written ideas), vocabulary lists, and early conferences with students (talking with children early on about their story ideas even before they have done much writing).[39] Allen Koshewa wrote, "Working with English language learners, I found that conferring early on, even if a student has written only a few sentences, helps relieve some of the pressure they feel."[40] In a non-graded, pressure-free environment like the library, it's possible that we can take advantage of our ability to remove even more of the intimidation that English language learners understandably feel about writing. The result is magical: a child learning the words she needs to express what *she* wants to express.

TOOLS FOR YOU

At the beginning of each chapter of this book, you will find an introduction to the Common Core State Standards that are promoted in that chapter's lessons. Each lesson is organized around one or more featured books, with a detailed summary. I've included a Public Relations Blurb (hereafter PR Blurb) in each lesson for use in designing your publicity or your flyers. The PR Blurbs cite the specific Common Core State Standards used in each lesson and can be used as "talking points" to help you explain the program to interested parents or teachers. In the past, I had a very generic flyer that invited kids to come and write, but I've learned that parents want more information when deciding whether to bring their kids to a program. The PR Blurb will show you what I typically share with parents.

Each lesson provides all the handouts you will need—you can copy and distribute them to the kids. Some lessons have extra handouts intended to support English language learners. For many of the lessons, we created special blank books that can be downloaded from alaeditions.org/webextras, printed, and photocopied. Kids love coming to the library to "write books," and they often show an intense motivation to fill every page. I usually create a sample book to model for them how easy and fun it is to fill those blank pages with their words and artwork. When they see what I've written, they are always more comfortable and confident about writing and sharing their writing. I strongly recommend this practice for anyone implementing these workshops, because when you create your own book, you get inside the mind of a child doing the workshop. It puts you in touch with your own inner child. Get to know that child, because that child is going to be your best advisor!

The structure of the workshops reflects my personal program planning style of mapping out blocks of time ranging from five to twenty minutes each. I like knowing that I have enough planned to fill an hour or an hour and a half. In each workshop, you will be teaching one or more lessons about language or literary devices. Parents are always happier when they see that at least one concrete fact or skill is being taught and modeled. Don't stress about the lessons, though—just try to make them simple and engaging, using the tips I have included for eliciting kids' active participation.

The supplies you will need for each program will vary somewhat, but for all the programs you will want to have either a whiteboard or flip chart pad, lots of tables and chairs for kids to write comfortably, and plenty of pencils, crayons, and markers. Any additional supplies you might need are listed at the beginning of the lesson.

TAKING THE LEAP

Perhaps you agree that more writing is needed in literacy programming, but you are still not ready to take the leap and start providing creative writing workshops for beginning readers. Librarians, you might have purchased this book to use it as a resource for the teachers you serve, but you may not think yourself ready to tackle the challenge of teaching this "active side of literacy."[41] My hope is that, after you see how fun and easy these writing programs are, your feelings will change. You'll catch the creative writing bug and start trying these suggestions as a way to encourage literacy. The results will be far-reaching, as you will watch kids of all backgrounds and abilities find new avenues for learning how to read, driven by their own desires and ideas. By giving kids more creative writing opportunities while they are still in the primary grades, we will create writers and readers who will be more likely to read proficiently by the third grade. We will improve the dismal statistics that show 68 percent of U.S. fourth graders not reading proficiently, because we will share with them the reading-writing connection—and we will start early on.[42]

For many children, their teachers might be the only adults they know who have ever asked them to write anything or showed them that writing can be fun, satisfying, and empowering. I hope that, after librarians have read this book, children will be able to add *librarians* to that list.

NOTES

1. OCLC, "Perceptions of Libraries, 2010: Context and Community," https://www.oclc.org/reports/2010perceptions.en.html.

2. Sarah Hinkle, "Every Child Ready to Read: Best Practices," *Children and Libraries* (2014): 35.

3. Ally Blumenfeld, "A Day in the Life of a Teen Writing Group," *The Library as Incubator Project* (blog), March 2016, www.libraryasincubatorproject.org/?p=18083.

4. James Moffett, introduction to *Collaboration through Writing and Reading,* edited by Anne H. Dyson (Urbana, IL: National Council of Teachers of English, 1989), 21–24.

5. Kay W. Cowan, "Bridging the Theme: The Arts and Emergent Literacy," *Primary Voices K–6* 9, no. 4 (2001): 11.

6. Sara Ackerman, "Becoming Writers in a Readers' World: Kindergarten Writing Journeys," *Language Arts* 93, no. 3 (2016): 201.

7. Jean Wallace Gillet and Lynn Beverly, *Directing the Writing Workshop: An Elementary Teacher's Handbook* (New York: Guilford Press, 2001), 33.

8. Ackerman, "Becoming Writers in a Readers' World: Kindergarten Writing Journeys," 201.

9. Nancy L. Anderson and Connie Briggs, "Reciprocity between Reading and Writing: Strategic Processing as Common Ground," *Reading Teacher* 64, no. 7 (2011): 548.

10. Ruth Culham, *The Writing Thief: Using Mentor Texts to Teach the Craft of Writing* (Newark, NJ: International Reading Association, 2014), 35.

11. Danling Fu and Jane S. Townsend, "'Serious' Learning: Language Lost," *Language Arts* 76, no. 5 (1999): 407.

12. Ibid., 408–9.

13. Lucy McCormick Calkins, *The Art of Teaching Writing* (Portsmouth, NH: Heinemann, 1986), 3–4.

14. Ackerman, "Becoming Writers in a Readers' World: Kindergarten Writing Journeys," 201.

15. Calkins, *The Art of Teaching Writing,* 38.

16. Ibid.

17. Gillet and Beverly, *Directing the Writing Workshop: An Elementary Teacher's Handbook,* 47.

18. Allen Koshewa, "Finding the Heartbeat: Applying Donald Graves's Approaches and Theories," *Language Arts* 89, no. 1 (2011): 52.

19. Calkins, *The Art of Teaching Writing*, 35.

20. Deborah Wells Rowe, Joanne Deal Fitch, and Alyson Smith Bass, "Toy Stories as Opportunities for Imagination and Reflection in Writer's Workshop," *Language Arts* 80, no. 5 (2003): 367–68.

21. Cowan, "Bridging the Theme: The Arts and Emergent Literacy," 14–15.

22. Rowe, Fitch, and Bass, "Toy Stories as Opportunities for Imagination and Reflection in Writer's Workshop," 367–68.

23. Eloise Andrade Laliberty and Maria E. Berzins, "Creating Opportunities for Emerging Biliteracy," *Primary Voices K–6* 8, no. 4 (2000): 13.

24. Calkins, *The Art of Teaching Writing*, 47.

25. James F. Swaim, "Laughing Together in Carnival: A Tale of Two Writers," *Language Arts* 79, no. 4 (2002): 342.

26. National Council of Teachers of English, "Professional Knowledge for the Teaching of Writing," www.ncte.org/positions/statements/teaching-writing.

27. Ibid.

28. American Association of School Librarians, "Position Statement on the School Librarian's Role in Reading," revised September 1, 2010, www.ala.org/aasl/advocacy/resources/statements/reading-role.

29. James R. Squire Office of Policy Research, "Reading and Writing across the Curriculum: One Implication of CCSS; Research-Based Recommendations for Fostering RAWAC." (Urbana, IL: National Council of Teachers of English, 2011), 15, www.theproecenter.info/uploads/2/2/5/5/22551316/reading_and_writing_across_the_curriculum.pdf.

30. Culham, *The Writing Thief: Using Mentor Texts to Teach the Craft of Writing*, 35.

31. Rachel L. Wadham and Terrell A. Young, *Integrating Children's Literature through the Common Core State Standards* (Santa Barbara, CA: Libraries Unlimited, 2015), 4.

32. Susan D. Martin and Sherry Dismuke, "Common Core: Missing the Mark for Writing Standards," *Language Arts* 93, no. 4 (2016): 303.

33. Common Core State Standards Initiative, "Key Shifts in English Language Arts," www.corestandards.org/other-resources/key-shifts-in-english-language-arts/.

34. Calkins, *The Art of Teaching Writing*, 25.

35. Roy Corden, "Developing Reading-Writing Connections: The Impact of Explicit Instruction of Literary Devices on the Quality of Children's Narrative Writing," *Journal of Research in Childhood Education* 21, no. 3 (2007): 285.

36. Nadeen T. Ruiz, Eleanor Vargas, and Angelica Beltran, "Becoming a Reader and Writer in a Bilingual Special Education Classroom," *Language Arts* 79, no. 4 (2002): 298–99.

37. Ibid., 306.

38. Ibid.

39. Ibid.

40. Koshewa, "Finding the Heartbeat: Applying Donald Graves's Approaches and Theories," 51–52.

41. Sarah Warshauer Freedman, Linda Flower, Glynda Hull, and J. R. Hayes, "Ten Years of Research: Achievements of the National Center for the Study of Writing and Literacy," National Writing Project (1995): 3, https://www.nwp.org/cs/public/print/nwpr/587.

42. Annie E. Casey Foundation, "Early Warning! Why Reading by the End of Third Grade Matters" (2010), www.aecf.org/resources/early-warning-why-reading-by-the-end-of-third-grade-matters/.

All You Need Is a
~~Good~~ TERRIBLE Idea

Some of the best and funniest picture books I have come across have sprung from the same kind of inspiration: *really bad ideas.* Children respond to books like that. Even children who may not think they have any good ideas worth sharing will notice right away when somebody else's idea completely defies logic. And they laugh because, for once, they are in a position of authority. For once, it is the adult who sounds silly. When you read *A Pig Parade Is a Terrible Idea* or *Teach Your Buffalo to Play Drums,* you put on the dunce hat for a little while, and everybody gets to revel in your folly. The playing field is then leveled, and children are emboldened to attempt some humor writing of their own.

STRETCH, ARGUE, AND PERSUADE

During most of the lessons in this chapter, children will be learning how to structure an argument. They will learn about basing an argument on supporting facts and using various tools of persuasive rhetoric. Kids will also learn about informative, how-to writing. They will be asked to give instructions for a ridiculous activity, requiring a stretch of the imagination and a suspension of disbelief.

They will also learn some tools of great creative writers and gain a greater understanding of what makes a story funny. They will learn editing skills so that they can craft every sentence they write to be more impactful. They will learn what irony is and how to build irony into a story.

It's important to spend a good amount of time in the brainstorming phase for these lessons, so that children are pushed to list all the possibilities suggested by the silly prompts. Good writing takes time, so I encourage you to use at least as much time as is recommended here, if not longer.

The skills of brainstorming, telling instructions in a sequence, and using persuasive rhetoric are all very important in developing the evidence-based informative and argumentative writing children will do in the upper grades.[1] Kids may be filling in word bubbles for a petulant alien or telling a story about something that could never happen in real life, but you will see them gain many real-world skills along the way.

COMMON CORE STANDARDS

CCSS.ELA-LITERACY.L.2.1.E: Use adjectives and adverbs, and choose between them depending on what is to be modified.

CCSS.ELA-LITERACY.L.2.1.F: Produce, expand, and rearrange complete simple and compound sentences (e.g., *The boy watched the movie; The little boy watched the movie; The action movie was watched by the little boy*).

CCSS.ELA-LITERACY.W.2.1: Write opinion pieces in which they introduce the topic or book they are writing about, state an opinion, supply reasons that support the opinion, use linking words (e.g., *because, and, also*) to connect opinion and reasons, and provide a concluding statement or section.

CCSS.ELA-LITERACY.W.2.2: Write informative/explanatory texts in which they introduce a topic, use facts and definitions to develop points, and provide a concluding statement or section.

CCSS.ELA-LITERACY.W.2.3: Write narratives in which they recount a well-elaborated event or short sequence of events, include details to describe actions, thoughts, and feelings, use temporal words to signal event order, and provide a sense of closure.

CCSS.ELA-LITERACY.W.2.5: With guidance and support from adults and peers, focus on a topic and strengthen writing as needed by revising and editing.

CCSS.ELA-LITERACY.RL.2.5: Describe the overall structure of a story, including describing how the beginning introduces the story and the ending concludes the action.

CCSS.ELA-LITERACY.RI.2.3: Describe the connection between a series of historical events, scientific ideas or concepts, or steps in technical procedures in a text.

A PANDA PARADE IS A TERRIBLE IDEA

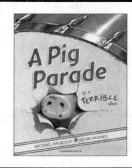

FEATURED BOOK

A Pig Parade Is a Terrible Idea
by Michael Ian Black,
illustrated by Kevin Hawkes

Length: About one hour

PR Blurb

After reading the book *A Pig Parade Is a Terrible Idea* by Michael Ian Black and illustrated by Kevin Hawkes, kids will write a picture book that argues a point, using details that show the contrasts between fantasy and reality. (**CCSS. ELA-LITERACY.W.2.1**)

In the book *A Pig Parade Is a Terrible Idea*, an unknown narrator explains why a parade of pigs would not be the wonderful spectacle the reader surely imagines it to be. Pigs won't put on uniforms, they won't march in formation—and music? Pigs would mess that up too, with sad country ballads. Nope, the narrator concludes, a pig parade would never work—but a panda parade . . . now *that* would be something!

Storytime (First Ten Minutes)

Have the kids sit on the floor and listen to you read *A Pig Parade Is a Terrible Idea* by Michael Ian Black and illustrated by Kevin Hawkes. After you finish reading, go back through the book and draw the kids' attention to Kevin Hawkes's illustrations. Ask the kids whether they notice any major differences between the first two pages. When the narrator is imagining how great a pig parade would be, the illustration style is cartoonlike, which contrasts sharply with the realistic paintings of pigs covered in filth.

Brainstorming (Next Ten Minutes)

Ask the kids to raise their hands and say what their favorite animals are. Write a few of the animals on the whiteboard or a large flip chart pad, and stop when you get to three or four (you won't have time to cover more than that). Now take one animal at a time and ask the children as a group to come up with reasons why that animal would, or wouldn't, be capable of putting on a good parade. Would the tigers eat the spectators? Would the hippos' snouts make good music stands? Would the pandas eat the clarinet reeds? Get silly with this, and try to keep going until the kids have come up with at least five suggestions for each animal. It may help the kids to make a list of things people do in parades.

Brainstorming (Next Thirty Minutes)

Have the children move to the tables, and give each child a copy of the handouts or the books downloaded from our website. One page of the handout contains suggested vocabulary and various "real" and "fantasy" images of animals, which the kids can cut out and use in their pictures. When I am really short on time, I give the kids sample images to work with so that they can spend more of their time writing. Make sure the children always have plenty of pencils, crayons, and markers.

Try not to emphasize spelling words correctly. Parents in the room might not understand; they might raise an eyebrow when you tell their children, "How do *you* think 'tiger' is spelled? *Tigr* works. I can read it. Keep on writing, don't stop!" Just as we do a lot of "parent patter" in our storytimes, modeling for parents how to make reading fun, we might sometimes have to explain to parents that we are following research-based models of promoting the child's own growing phonographic awareness. Or you could just say gently, "Today, we're not focusing on spelling accuracy. We are focusing more on ideas and imagination. Invented spellings are okay, and they actually show a lot of growth."

If you are working with English language learners, I recommend scaffolding their writing by modeling a few sentences on your whiteboard or flip chart pad. This strategy will show the children some of the conventions of English and help them set up a sentence that argues a point. Here are some examples:

> **You might think that a panda parade would be cool.**
> **But you're wrong, because the pandas would eat all the woodwind instruments!**
>
> You might think that a tiger parade would be _____ .
> But in the real world, a tiger parade would be _____ !
> The tigers would _____ !

In these examples, you're teaching the children that a good argument demonstrates awareness of the opposing viewpoint and then shows direct evidence why that viewpoint would be wrong. The kids will learn the back and forth pattern of "You might think . . . but that's wrong because . . . ."

This lesson also includes a list of parade vocabulary words that you can have on hand during the writing program for kids who are really struggling. Just remember that if the kids are fluent in English, it is best to push them to increase that fluency by sounding out the words and writing them down without too much help.

Storytime (Last Ten Minutes)

Have all the kids return to where they were sitting earlier when you read the picture book, and tell them you're going to have a storytime with the books that they wrote. Invite the kids to sit in the storyteller's chair with their books and read their writing to the whole group. Never insist that children share their writing; always emphasize that this part is totally optional. Most children, seeing peers share their work, will be eager for their own turn to share. But some children will be very uncomfortable reading their books out loud, and forcing them to do so might cause them to feel uncomfortable about writing, too.

For many kids (and their parents), this is the most magical part of the program. During this storytime, each child has a chance to transform herself from audience to storyteller, from reader to author. Make sure the kids are listening quietly when their peers are reading. I find that it helps to have kids sit on the floor while the person reading is sitting in a chair in front of them.

Applaud their writing! Be the first one to point out something you liked about their arguments. Invite kids in the audience to comment about the things they liked, too.

Mark Twain said, "I can live for two months on a good compliment." But children don't just "live" on compliments—they thrive and grow.

TITLE: A _____ Parade Is a _____ Idea.

BY: _____

_____

_____

_____

_____

Which Illustrations Are Realistic? Which Are Fantasy?

Not Real (Fiction)   Real (Non-Fiction)

Marching Band Gear

Vocabulary You Can Try

great	instruments	conductor	disaster
clarinet	saxophone	incapable	balloons
eat	horribly	cymbals	baton twirler
terrible	musicians	announcer	fantastic
trombone	piccolo	terrific	lopsided
terrifically	beautifully	flute	cheerleader
tuba	stupendous	haphazard	catastrophe
horrifically	bass drum	banner	audience
because	badly	horrible	grand marshal
trumpet	ridiculous	float	uniform
wonderfully	snare drum	drum major	march

IF YOU EVER WANT TO BRING A SHARK TO THE PARK, DON'T

FEATURED BOOK	ALTERNATE BOOK
If You Ever Want to Bring a Piano to the Beach, DON'T! by Elise Parsley	*If You Ever Want to Bring an Alligator to School, DON'T!* by Elise Parsley

Length: About one hour

PR Blurb

After reading the book *If You Ever Want to Bring a Piano to the Beach, DON'T!* by Elise Parsley, kids will work together in groups to write and illustrate a story with irony. (**CCSS.ELA-LITERACY.W.2.2, CCSS.ELA-LITERACY.W.2.3**)

In the book *If You Ever Want to Bring a Piano to the Beach, DON'T!* by Elise Parsley, a little girl named Magnolia teaches us the dos and don'ts of lugging a giant percussion instrument to the beach, because she has learned the hard way that "you might lose it." "How does one manage to lose a *piano* at the beach?," you may well wonder. First, you will need to hear Magnolia's instructions for getting the piano there, rolling it on your little brother's wagon. After a series of misadventures, the piano will get dirty—so you push it out into the ocean, and that's how you lose it. In the end, Magnolia learns her lesson, as do we. But, happily, Magnolia learns something else, too—that if you bring a piano to the beach, "you never know what you might find."

Storytime (First Ten Minutes)

Read *If You Ever Want to Bring a Piano to the Beach, DON'T!* by Elise Parsley. After reading, talk about the book. Remind the kids what Magnolia's mother said, and ask if they thought the idea of losing a piano at the beach made any sense at first. Ask if they were surprised when the very thing her mother warned her about actually does happen. Then introduce today's vocabulary word: *irony*.

Brainstorming: Things That DON'T Go Together (Next Ten Minutes)

Elise Parsley's Magnolia Says DON'T series places things in settings where they would never fit in real life, like an alligator at an elementary school or a piano at the beach. Before your program, on a sheet of your flip chart pad or a part of your whiteboard, write the following scenes that kids will be familiar with:

Park	Opera house	Swimming pool
Doctor's office	Baseball game	Mall
Library	Ice skating rink	Museum
Concert		

Add any other settings you can think of, and during this time in the program ask the kids to think of more settings to add. Next, ask the kids to help you write down one animal, person, or object that would *not* fit in each setting. Your list will start to look something like this:

- » Park—A shark
- » Doctor's office—A giraffe
- » Library—A megaphone
- » Concert—A pirate
- » Opera house—Your baby brother
- » Baseball game—A hippopotamus
- » Swimming pool—Your computer

You might decide to stop there and have the kids write stories about those pairings. I recommend that approach for a group that is either very young or has a lot of English language learners. But if you think the kids are able to learn more of the fundamentals of writing stories with irony, the next part of this lesson addresses that aspect.

Brainstorming: "You'd Better Not . . ." (Next Ten Minutes)

Magnolia's mother allows her to take the piano to the beach as long as she doesn't lose it. Using the whiteboard or flip chart pad, help the children list things that their moms or dads might warn them about. I recommend writing a few on the board first to show the kids what you mean:

"You'd better not catch a cold."
"You'd better not spoil your dinner."
"As long as you're not late for school."
"As long as you don't poke your eye out."

Invite the kids to add more warnings, ultimata, or conditions that their parents would give them before allowing them to do something they want to do. Then talk to the kids about irony and how surprising it is when Magnolia manages to lose a piano at the beach. (It's not like the piano blends into the scenery!)

Brainstorming (Next Thirty Minutes)

I encourage you to have the kids form groups for this writing activity or at least work in pairs. After the kids are seated at the writing tables and have chosen partners, distribute the handouts (or the books downloaded from our website and folded and stapled following the instructions in appendix A). Tell each group to choose one pairing of things that don't fit and one parental warning. Their story will be about the warning coming true.

This kind of writing, using an author's formula as a guide, will push kids to write a conclusion for their stories. It will be challenging for some, but two things that children at this age have to learn are how to "provide a concluding statement" (**CCSS.ELA-LITERACY.W.2.2**) and a "sense of closure" (**CCSS.ELA-LITERACY.W.2.3**). It takes a lot of practice for any writer to learn how to wrap everything up, but it's an important skill not just for narrative writing but for informational and persuasive writing as well.

Tips for Working with English Language Learners

If you are working with English language learners, encourage them to write their parents' warnings exactly as their parents would say them in their native language. When you do that, you teach kids that their native languages are just as valid and important to master as English, and you celebrate their cultural diversity. That respect for "who students are, and who their families are" is important, and when we validate children's native languages, we show them that being bilingual and biliterate are strengths to be proud of.[2]

Storytime (Last Ten Minutes)

Have all the children sit on the floor and then ask whether any of them would like to share their stories. Invite them to take turns reading what their groups wrote.

 AREN'T FORMULAS *BAD*?

What's so creative about writing to a formula?, you might wonder. It's natural for writing teachers to have a love–hate relationship with formulas. We want children to learn how art is made, but we don't want to run the risk of dissuading children from creating their own inventive new forms. We also want to make sure children are given opportunities to write whatever they want so that they aren't made to be "more the consumers of others' thinking than original thinkers themselves."[a]

I understand that viewpoint completely, but I have also seen a lot of good come from learning about writing with formulas. Writers have been trying to find formulas for what makes a good story ever since Aristotle. Sometimes those formulas can provide a set of parameters to guide creation. When writers write within parameters, the creative process becomes more of an inward exploration as authors make the structure their own and probe how deep the parameters go. Sometimes the formula simply works as a talisman to guard against writer's block. There's a reason the Magnolia Says DON'T books, the If You Give a Mouse a Cookie books, and the Don't Let the Pigeon Drive the Bus! books are so formulaic and so *prolific*: each author has hit upon something that *works* and does not need to reinvent the wheel.

Just as you want students in science classes to learn the laws of physics and test them out in experiments, you want your writing students to learn the mechanics of what makes a good joke funny or what makes a story entertaining. Some exposure to formulas in mentor texts will therefore be necessary. As long as teachers give their students plenty of other daily opportunities for writing anything they want without templates or prompts, one prompt a week will not kill children's creativity. It will simply push them to try something they haven't tried before.

a. James Moffett, *Introduction to Collaboration through Writing and Reading*, edited by Anne H. Dyson (Urbana, IL: National Council of Teachers of English, 1989), 21–24.

TITLE: _____
_____

BY: _____

If you ever want to _____,
your parents will probably say:

_____

_____

Of course, you'll do it anyway, but you'll make sure to _____
because:

_____

_____

Don't forget to show the reader how your parents' warning came true!

_____

_____

_____

Write a conclusion: Did your character learn anything from this experience?

_____

_____

_____

REVISING AND ILLUSTRATING
Smartphones Are Definitely <u>Not</u> for Animals

3

FEATURED BOOK

Animals Should Definitely <u>Not</u> Wear Clothing
by Judi Barrett, illustrated by Ron Barrett

Length: About one hour

Supplies

» Photocopier (on hand for the program)
» Stapler

Draft sentences for kids to rewrite, copied and cut into folded strips for distribution (there are a total of twenty, so if you have more than twenty children, you could make two copies of each page and create two books).

PR Blurb

After reading the book *Animals Should Definitely <u>Not</u> Wear Clothing* by Judi Barrett and illustrated by Ron Barrett, kids will work together to write and illustrate a funny book about animals while learning about understatement, revision, and illustration. (**CCSS.ELA-LITERACY.W.2.1, CCSS.ELA-LITERACY.W.2.2, CCSS.ELA-LITERACY.W.2.5, CCSS.ELA-LITERACY.L.2.1.F**)

Judi and Ron Barrett's classic picture book makes a very persuasive argument about the disasters that would ensue if animals wore clothes. The pictures in the book do the heavy lifting, while the text is wonderfully sparse. We learn why pants were not made with snakes or hens in mind by seeing the snake slither out of them and the hen's egg get stuck in them. Animal by animal, the Barretts demonstrate why clothes should be reserved for humans (like the portly lady pictured at the end, who one hopes will never have to endure the embarrassment of seeing an actual elephant wearing the same outfit she has on).

Storytime (First Ten Minutes)

Invite the children to sit on the floor while you read to them the book *Animals Should Definitely <u>Not</u> Wear Clothing* by Judi Barrett and illustrated by Ron Barrett. As you read, point out how the pictures in the book do most of the heavy lifting. Keep in mind that it is rarely obvious to a child how an illustrator plans out the pictures in good books. Children are often surprised to learn that illustrators don't just draw whatever they want but think very carefully about how their drawing is going to contribute to the meaning of the words.[3] You will see your writing students' own illustrations change once they understand the kind of thoughtful planning that goes into professional illustrations.

Talk about how brief the text is and how little it manages to say while actually saying a lot. Then introduce the vocabulary word for today: *understatement*. Explain to the kids that in humor writing, less is more.

Group Writing (Next Twenty Minutes)

Tell the group that you have been trying hard to write a book that's funny like Judi and Ron Barrett's, except that your book is not funny yet. Your book is about why animals shouldn't use phones. Perhaps the kids can help you rewrite it and illustrate it, and you can all publish it together as author-illustrators!

On the flip chart, show the kids a sentence you have written:

> *Phones are definitely not for snakes because a snake doesn't have fingers, so it will be impossible for a snake to send text messages.*

Ask the kids to help you rewrite the sentence to be shorter and funnier and to rely more on a funny illustration to carry the meaning. Explain that fewer words, in this case, would be better. Then ask the children to vote: what part of the sentence should be removed? You could separate parts of the sentence so that it looks like this:

a. Phones are definitely not for snakes because
b. a snake doesn't have fingers, so
c. it will be impossible for a snake to send text messages.

Ask the kids which part of the sentence is redundant or unnecessary. Which part of the sentence could be better shown with a funny picture—a, b, or c?

Whichever part of the sentence the kids suggest removing first, rewrite the sentence without it. Then ask them to raise their hands if they have an idea for a further rewrite that would harness the power of understatement. Remind them that "less is more." Obviously texting would be impossible for a snake. But what if a snake didn't know that? What if a snake really wanted to send someone a text message and couldn't figure out how to do it? Well, you might then be able to make the understatement that texting would be *hard* for a snake.

Write down any understated sentences the kids suggest. Then draw (or ask a volunteer to draw) a snake looking at a cell phone. (Do you know why I love doing this exercise with a snake? Because *anyone* can draw a snake, including me.) Draw a thought bubble next to the snake, and ask the kids what the snake might be thinking. Maybe the snake is thinking, "Great—now my friend will think I am ignoring her." Or maybe it's thinking, "If only I had tentacles like my friend Octopus." See what the kids come up with and fill in the thought bubble.

Individual Writing (Next Twenty Minutes) ·······························

Have the children sit at the tables, and pass out the handouts. Tell the children that they are going to help rewrite and illustrate one page about why animals can't use phones. Then you will put all the children's pages together in a book.

Each child will receive a "draft" sentence printed on a slip of paper, which you'll want to prepare ahead of time. Draft sentences can be found on the next few pages. The children then will try to write a better sentence on the handout and draw an illustration. You can make distributing the draft sentences fun by putting them in a basket and having each child draw one slip of paper at random. Alternatively, you can invite the kids to take a few minutes to review all the slips and choose one that resonates with them.

If you have kids who would prefer to write something completely original, that's fine! Just be sure to give them plenty of time and perhaps plan for the possibility by increasing the length of the workshop.

Encourage the kids to go over the top with their illustrations and be minimal with their words. For this exercise the children are going for really *short* sentences that pack a lot of humor into a small clump of words. If they finish early, you could give them another page and another sentence to rewrite. When they are finished, staple their pages together into a book. Try to have a photocopier available so that (time permitting) each participant can receive a copy of the book to take home.

Storytime (Last Ten Minutes) ·······························

Ask the kids to return to the floor where they sat earlier while you read *Animals Should Definitely Not Wear Clothing*. Invite the children to take turns reading the pages that they wrote and illustrated. Put the book in a place of honor like a Young Authors shelf so that kids can read it whenever they like!

DRAFT SENTENCES FOR KIDS TO REWRITE (cut along the dotted lines)

A deer can't use a smartphone because deer have hooves, and the hooves are rough and would probably break the screen.

A dog would carry the phone around in its mouth, getting the phone all wet with slobber. This will break the phone and ruin the electrical connections.

A pig would probably drop the phone in the mud and lose it. You would try calling your phone to find it, but it would be so full of mud that it wouldn't ring anymore.

A giraffe wouldn't be able to take selfies. It would need someone to invent a selfie stick that is at least fifteen feet tall, because otherwise its face would never come out in photos.

A parrot would call your grandmother and make her very upset by copying everything she says in a silly voice.

A cat would find your favorite cat videos on YouTube and then the cat would hoard your phone and you would never see your phone again.

A pelican would put the phone in its throat pouch and then forget it is there until the phone starts ringing, and the pelican would freak out because it wouldn't know what was doing that.

A sloth would take forever to return your phone calls because sloths are very slow animals.

A koala would never pick up the phone because it would always be sleeping, and you would never be sure when it was a safe time to call.

An eagle might see the picture of your pet guinea pig and think there was a real guinea pig in there. It would drop the phone from a great height to get the guinea pig out, and the phone would break.

A songbird would be very confused by the sounds coming out of the phone every time it rings, looking around for the bird that is making all that weird noise.

A walrus wouldn't be able to dial the right number because of its enormous flippers, so it would keep getting wrong numbers.

A mole wouldn't be able to see anything on the screen, so it would keep dialing wrong numbers.

A peacock would fill up all your space with selfies because peacocks are very vain.

An oyster would not be able to use the phone because an oyster doesn't have eyes and doesn't have ears.

A spectacled bear would need extra spectacles to read the tiny print of the websites, and he would look so silly that all his friends would make fun of him.

A snapping turtle wouldn't need a phone because she is so mean and critical of her friends that she no longer has anyone to talk to.

A starfish would have to take its mouth out of the dirt before it would be able to talk on the phone, or its friends won't be able to hear it.

A howler monkey would spend so much time screaming about this and whining about that that you'll wish you'd never given it a phone.

A snake doesn't have fingers, so it would be impossible for it to send text messages.

On the lines above, rewrite the sentence you were given and draw a picture.
Make your sentence as short and understated as possible!

This page written and illustrated by:

_____

DON'T LET THE ALIEN PLAY IN THE TOILET!

FEATURED BOOK	ALTERNATE BOOKS
The Pigeon Needs a Bath! by Mo Willems 	**Don't Let the Pigeon Drive the Bus!** by Mo Willems **Don't Let the Pigeon Stay Up Late!** by Mo Willems **The Pigeon Wants a Puppy!** by Mo Willems

Length: About one hour and fifteen minutes

PR Blurb

After reading the book *The Pigeon Needs a Bath!* by Mo Willems, kids will learn about persuasive rhetoric and the concepts of logos, ethos, and pathos. Then they will write a story in which a character uses those three kinds of rhetoric to convince the reader of something. (**CCSS.ELA-LITERACY.W.2.1, CCSS. ELA-LITERACY.W.2.5, CCSS.ELA-LITERACY.L.2.6**)

In the petulant Pigeon who is frustrated at never getting his way, Mo Willems has created a character that children can relate to. The books make outstanding read-alouds because the Pigeon has a flair for drama, bouncing from one emotion to the next with incredible speed. The Pigeon begs, cajoles, cries, makes promises, and attempts many kinds of rhetoric to get his way, but, in the end, he generally adapts to his situation with resilience, as any child who has ever sat in time-out for having a tantrum has had to learn to do. What librarians love about the Pigeon books, and the reason they are featured so often in our storytimes, is that they elevate the child to the position of The Grownup Who Knows What Is Best, giving the child a rare opportunity to tell someone else "No!"

Storytime (First Ten Minutes)

Have the children sit on the floor and listen while you read the book *The Pigeon Needs a Bath!* by Mo Willems. When you're finished, go back through the book and ask the kids how many different kinds of arguments they think the Pigeon used to try to convince them that he didn't need a bath. They might say "ten" or "twenty" or "a hundred," but tell them he actually uses variations of three: ethos, pathos, and logos. Then go right into the lesson.

Lesson on Types of Rhetoric (Next Fifteen Minutes) ·····················

Put these words on the board or flip chart: *ethos, pathos, logos*. You may also wish to write the word *rhetoric* and explain what rhetoric is. Merriam-Webster defines it as "the art of speaking or writing effectively," especially "as a means of communication or persuasion."

Explain to the kids that *ethos* is a Greek word meaning a demonstration of credibility, trustworthiness, or strong character. People will often listen to you if they think you are a good person worth trusting. When the Pigeon says life is short and asks, "Why waste it on unimportant things?," he is acting like a philosopher and like he has a solid philosophical basis for his decision not to bathe. He maintains that "it's a very normal smell, for a pigeon," asserting himself as the authority on how pigeons should smell. He is using a form of rhetoric that the Greeks called *ethos*.

With the help of the kids, brainstorm some other common, everyday examples they hear of people using ethos and write the examples underneath that word. If the children have trouble, you can suggest a few expressions that are frequently used by young arguers like them:

> » "You can't tell me what to do! You're not my mom!"
> » "Teacher said so!"
> » "If you do this for me, I'll be your best friend."

Next, explain that *pathos* means an appeal to the listener's emotions or sometimes a manipulation of a person's emotions. When the Pigeon says, "If it means soooooooo much to you," he is trying to make the reader feel guilty about making him take a bath. Ask the kids if they can think of any other ways that people use emotional manipulation to get what they want. You can suggest a few common arguments of pathos, such as the following:

> » "Don't you love me? Don't you want me to be happy?"
> » "You wouldn't deny a poor little kid like me the thing I have been wishing for since practically forever . . . would you?"

Finally, explain that *logos* is a Greek word meaning an argument that appeals to reason, using facts and logic. When the Pigeon says, "You know, in some places it is impolite to bathe," he is doing his best to steer the conversation in such a way that he can use "facts" to persuade the reader that baths are not important. Ask the kids if they can think of any other examples from the book where the Pigeon uses logos. You can help them by reminding them of these examples:

» "That is a matter of opinion."
» "I don't really need a bath. I took one last month."
» "Clean, dirty, they're just words, right?"

Brainstorming (Next Ten Minutes)

Using a new sheet or a new place on the whiteboard, ask the kids to brainstorm things that their parents tell them they are *not* allowed to do or things that their parents tell them they *have* to do. These can be things like the following:

» "You have to eat your vegetables."
» "Don't write on the wall!"

Ask whether the kids have any younger siblings, and whether they've ever been told not to let their siblings do something, like the following:

» "Don't let the baby play with your markers!"
» "Don't let the baby put his hands in the toilet!"

Writing (Next Twenty-Five Minutes)

Have the kids take a seat at the tables and choose from the list of parent commands. In this exercise they will create an argumentative character like the Pigeon. If they want to, they can draw their own character or draw Willems's Pigeon, or they can cut and glue the little alien pictures you will provide. Pass out the handouts (or books downloaded from our website), and ask the kids to write the dialogue bubbles for the alien or the other character. Encourage the children to use what they know about the Pigeon's use of rhetoric to write the things their characters will say. Their characters should beg and cajole and argue, using ethos, logos, and pathos.

Wherever needed, give the children mini-lessons on dialogue, punctuation, and voice. Make sure the kids understand that they should always write the speech bubbles from the main character's point of view.

If you are working with English language learners, give them a lot of scaffolding and model sentences for them on the whiteboard. With appropriate modeling this lesson will be very good to do with English language learners because it is designed to build on their growing conversational skills. Give English language learners plenty of personal attention to help them write the alien's speech bubbles with appropriate expressions of anger, frustration, and joy. Here are some examples of model sentences:

I know what I'm doing. I've _____ lots of times. (*ethos*)

Won't you be nice and let me _____ ? (*pathos*)

Nothing bad is going to happen. In fact, _____. (*logos*)

Storytime (Last Ten Minutes)

Ask the kids to take a seat again on the floor and invite them one by one to read their stories in the same chair you sat in. See if the kids can point out each author's use of ethos, pathos, and logos! Encourage the kids to comment on whatever they liked about their peers' words or illustrations.

TITLE:
_____

BY:
_____

ALIENS YOU CAN CUT AND PASTE

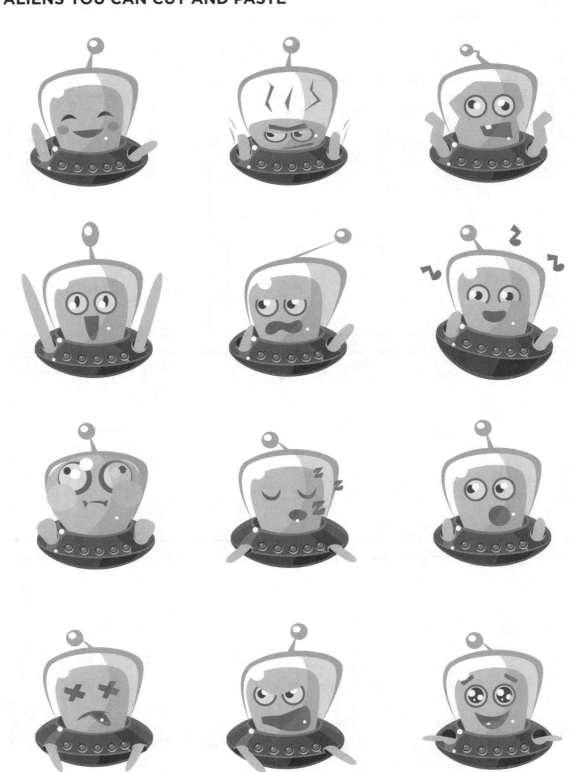

TEACH YOUR ZEBRA TO RIDE A BIKE

FEATURED BOOK	ALTERNATE BOOK
Teach Your Buffalo to Play Drums by Audrey Vernick, illustrated by Daniel Jennewein	***Is Your Buffalo Ready for Kindergarten?*** by Audrey Vernick, illustrated by Daniel Jennewein

Length: About one hour

PR Blurb

After reading *Teach Your Buffalo to Play Drums* by Audrey Vernick and illustrated by Daniel Jennewein, kids will write an instruction manual for teaching an animal to do something that kids can do, step by hilarious step. (**CCSS.ELA-LITERACY.W.2.2, CCSS.ELA-LITERACY.RI.2.3**)

It may seem impossible to teach a hooved animal like a buffalo to play the drums, but Audrey Vernick's friendly, gentle instructions will show you that it can be done! Vernick's Buffalo books written in the second person put the child reader in the role of the teacher. Jennewein's pictures depict a very appealing, sympathetic character who just needs a little support and encouragement. Give these books to any child who has ever felt unable to master something "impossible"—Vernick and Jennewein will show that, with a little confidence and a caring friend or teacher, nothing is impossible!

Storytime (First Ten Minutes)

Have the children sit on the floor and listen as you read *Teach Your Buffalo to Play Drums*. After reading, ask them if they've ever had to learn how to do something that seemed impossible. Did they ever master it? How? Could they explain to a younger kid how to do it now that they are good at it?

Brainstorming (Next Ten Minutes)

Using the board or flip chart, ask the kids to help you make a list of things they know how to do. They should especially focus on things they could teach someone else to do.

Now pick one skill and, on a new sheet or a new section of the board or flip chart, ask the kids to help you list all the steps that one would need to do to acquire that skill. Be sure to use words such as *first* and *next* and *then*. Sequence is a very important part of the writing skills needed for this lesson.

The children can also help you make a list of animals to choose from for writing their stories. You can ask each child, "What's your favorite animal?" and then put it on the board or flip chart.

Writing (Next Thirty Minutes)

Have the children sit at the tables, and pass out the handouts or the folded and stapled books you download from our website. Invite the kids to choose any animal and any skill, whether it's on the board or not. They will write about the step-by-step process of teaching that animal to do something hard for an animal. As they write, the kids should consider *why* it would be difficult for that animal and how they would explain the process using directions that accommodate the animal's body and physical abilities.

Put the following words on the whiteboard or flip chart pad to help the children think about the physical aspects of animals that make them different from humans and that therefore might pose certain physical limitations:

» Hooves	» Snout	» Antlers
» Paws	» Trunk	» Tails
» Claws	» Horns	

Storytime (Last Ten Minutes)

Have the children return to their earlier spots on the floor and invite them to come up to the storyteller's chair one by one and read their instruction manuals to the group. Applaud them and focus on how well they described the steps to take or the sequence of steps. After this exercise, kids should feel like not only very knowledgeable and capable individuals but brilliant writers as well!

NOTES

1. Common Core State Standards Initiative, "Key Shifts in English Language Arts," www.corestandards.org/other-resources/key-shifts-in-english-language-arts/.
2. Dan Lukiv, "Home-Grown Publishing, Part Two: How to Develop a Creative Writing Program," CanTeach, accessed December 2, 2016, www.canteach.ca/elementary/createwrite10.html.
3. Jean Wallace Gillet and Lynn Beverly, *Directing the Writing Workshop: An Elementary Teacher's Handbook* (New York: Guilford Press, 2001), 172.

TITLE: _____

BY: _____

What are you going to teach your animal to do? What will be the hardest thing about it?

_____

_____

_____

Step 1: _____

_____

Step 2: _____

_____

Step 3: _____

_____

Step 4: _____

_____

Step 5: _____

_____

Step 6: _____

_____

Step 7: _____

_____

Step 8: _____

_____

Step 9: _____

_____

Step 10: _____

_____

CHAPTER

THREE

Fractured Fairy Tales

airy tales provide a valuable source of inspiration for writers because they give us a shared culture that we can draw from so that readers can easily connect with our stories. Fairy tales give us stock characters and stories that have been retold in countless ways and that share similarities across cultures. As a result, fairy tales are a valuable tool for teaching children that literature is not something old and dead but something *alive*, a conversation in which readers and writers are continually invited to contribute new layers of meaning.

NEW MEANING FROM OLD STORIES

During most of the lessons in this chapter, children will be learning how to retell an old story and make it uniquely their own. They will learn characterization and character perspective, giving life to familiar characters whose stories they may have taken for granted before. They will analyze the problems for those characters and understand how conflict drives characters to act and propels stories to take shape. By rewriting familiar fairy tales with changes to the characters and settings, they will demonstrate how those elements can impact the outcome of a story. They will learn that fairy tales and fables have a plot that sets up a problem and ends with some sort of lesson learned, and they will practice telling stories with that basic structure.

COMMON CORE STANDARDS

CCSS.ELA-LITERACY.L.2.1.E: Use adjectives and adverbs, and choose between them depending on what is to be modified.

CCSS.ELA-LITERACY.W.2.3: Write narratives in which they recount a well-elaborated event or short sequence of events, include details to describe actions, thoughts, and feelings, use temporal words to signal event order, and provide a sense of closure.

CCSS.ELA-LITERACY.W.2.5: With guidance and support from adults and peers, focus on a topic and strengthen writing as needed by revising and editing.

CCSS.ELA-LITERACY.RL.2.2: Recount stories, including fables and folktales from diverse cultures, and determine their central message, lesson, or moral.

CCSS.ELA-LITERACY.RL.2.3: Describe how characters in a story respond to major events and challenges.

CCSS.ELA-LITERACY.RL.2.5: Describe the overall structure of a story, including describing how the beginning introduces the story and the ending concludes the action.

CCSS.ELA-LITERACY.RL.2.6: Acknowledge differences in the points of view of characters, including by speaking in a different voice for each character when reading dialogue aloud.

THE VERY OLD BAD WOLF

FEATURED BOOK

Very Little Red Riding Hood
by Teresa Heapy and Sue Heap

Length: About one hour

PR Blurb

After reading *Very Little Red Riding Hood* by Teresa Heapy and Sue Heap, kids will rewrite familiar fairy tales while exploring how changing one aspect of one character can change a story completely. (**CCSS.ELA-LITERACY.RL.2.2, CCSS.ELA-LITERACY.W.2.3, CCSS.ELA-LITERACY.L.2.1.E**)

Very Little Red Riding Hood by Heapy and Heap tells a familiar fairy tale with a twist: instead of being a young lady, Red Riding Hood is reenvisioned as a fearless toddler with a winning openness and a guileless heart. She goes through the woods with a toddler's naive confidence that nothing can harm her. But she is a gutsy toddler, too! She has no difficulty bossing the Big Bad Wolf around, but she has even less difficulty making him her new friend and playmate. Her kindness tames the Big Bad Wolf, and nobody gets eaten. It seems that changing her from "Little" to "Very Little" makes a very *big* difference in her story!

Storytime (First Ten Minutes)

Have the children sit on the floor and listen as you read *Very Little Red Riding Hood*. After reading, ask the kids how changing Red Riding Hood's age changed the story. How old do they think Little Red Riding Hood is in the original story? How does rewriting her character as a toddler change the attitudes, motivations, and actions of the other characters, like the grandma and the wolf?

Brainstorming (Next Ten Minutes)

Using the flip chart or board, invite the kids to help you make a list of fairy-tale characters or nursery rhyme characters by raising their hands and suggesting any characters that come to mind. Then next to each character's name, write some basic characteristics of that character. You could start with the following:

- » Age
- » Size
- » Boy or girl
- » Human or animal
- » Special skills
- » Diet
- » Looks
- » Personality

This list will give you a rough sketch of who each character is and how the characters function in relation to other characters in their fairy-tale stories.

Now ask the kids to help you circle the one characteristic that might change the course of the fairy tale by making the character different enough to impact the way that character interacts with others. You could take a vote on which characteristic to circle for each character. It's important to do lots of talking about the possible repercussions of this change, because while kids are talking, their ideas grow.

Writing (Next Thirty Minutes)

Have the children sit at the tables, and pass out either the handouts included or the books that you can download from our website. Encourage the kids to choose one of the characters from the brainstorming exercise or any other fairy-tale character they like and rewrite their stories with a major change to one of the traits that defines that character. Changing the characters will change their stories.

Storytime (Last Ten Minutes)

Ask the kids to return to their spots on the floor where they listened to you read *Very Little Red Riding Hood.* Invite them to take turns sitting in the storyteller's chair and reading their new versions of fairy tales. Praise them for the ways in which they have taken the original story and rewritten it so that a small change made a big difference.

TITLE: _____

BY: _____

Start by telling the fairy tale as usual, and then introduce the twist!

_____

_____

_____

_____

_____

FAIRY-TALE CHARACTERS ON VACATION

The Three Pigs
by David Wiesner

Length: About one hour

PR Blurb

After reading *The Three Pigs* by David Wiesner, kids will write about fairy-tale characters escaping from their stories, including consideration for why the character might want to escape and what that character would rather be doing. (**CCSS.ELA-LITERACY.RL.2.2, CCSS.ELA-LITERACY.RL.2.6, CCSS.ELA-LITERACY.W.2.3**)

It's easy to see why David Wiesner won the Caldecott Medal for his out-of-the-box, beautifully drawn book *The Three Pigs*. Their fairy tale starts off as usual except for one thing—they realize they don't very much like their story with the bullying wolf who blows down their houses. They decide to escape and discover it's as easy as jumping out of the pages and into the pages of a different book. They find themselves in other fairy tales, and they bring other characters away with them to fly away on paper airplanes to find a better life.

Storytime (First Ten Minutes)

Have the kids sit on the floor and listen as you read *The Three Pigs*. Ask them why they think the pigs would want to leave their story. Would you want to leave if you were being harassed and threatened by an angry wolf? In many fairy tales, someone is hunted or eaten. Why are those fairy tales so grim? Does good always prevail in fairy tales? Do innocent people suffer?

Brainstorming (Next Ten Minutes)

Help the kids write down on the board or flip chart a list of fairy-tale characters they know from books or films. But leave plenty of space between each name because you will be doing more writing about each character.

Next to each name, write one major problem the character has. Does she get hunted by an evil queen? Eaten by a wolf? Sent away by her parents to starve in the woods?

Now, underneath each character's name and problem, write something the character likes. If kids don't know what a character likes, encourage them to make up something. Disney added a love of music and dancing to its Three Little Pigs characters. Maybe what Red Riding Hood's Granny would really love, more than cookies or a bottle of wine, is to relax on a warm beach far away from the woods! Then kids will start to see that they could write a story sending Granny to the Bahamas for a while. ("Granny, how tan your skin has grown!" "The better to protect it from UV rays, my dear.") Brainstorm some possible places where characters could travel to achieve their dream vacations.

Writing (Next Thirty Minutes)

Have the kids take a seat at the tables, and pass out the worksheets or books. Invite the children to tell a story about what might happen if a fairy-tale character went on vacation. Why would that character want to leave? Where would he go? What would he do? What would happen to the other characters who had to continue with their stories?

Storytime (Last Ten Minutes)

Ask the kids to return to their places on the floor where you read *The Three Pigs*. Invite them to sit in the storyteller's chair one by one and read their creations!

Hello, my name is _____ **, and, as you can see,
I'm not in my story anymore. It was about time I went on vacation.**

Why did this person leave the fairy tale?

_____

_____

_____

_____

Does this person meet anyone from other fairy tales? Do they become friends?
What if they don't like each other?

_____

_____

_____

While this person is away, does another character get left behind? Will that character
miss the person who left?

_____

_____

_____

DOUBLE TROUBLE

FEATURED BOOK

Two of Everything
by Lily Toy Hong

Length: About one hour

PR Blurb

After reading *Two of Everything* by Lily Toy Hong, kids will write their own versions of this Chinese fairy tale. They will learn about plot and create a story that takes a wild, imaginative premise and follows it to its logical conclusion. (**CCSS.ELA-LITERACY.RL.2.2, CCSS.ELA-LITERACY.W.2.3**)

The endearing old couple in Lily Toy Hong's *Two of Everything* live a life of few luxuries in China, working the land and bringing their small harvest to the village market. After the husband brings home a large pot he found there, they accidentally discover that the pot duplicates anything they put in it. The two old people exhibit a very understandable and childlike haste as they gleefully throw things into the pot to make two of everything. But their joy turns to shock when they fall in and duplicate themselves! By the end of the story you might expect them to bury the pot or dread its power, as would probably happen in a European fairy tale, but they aren't as extreme as all that—they just need to be careful with it, that's all! One of the things I love about this story is how pure and innocent the characters are. Even when their circumstances change drastically and they go from poverty to wealth, they remain the same charming and harmonious people. After all, you have to admire a couple who can be such good friends with their clones!

Storytime and a What If Discussion (First Ten Minutes)

Have the kids sit on the floor and listen while you read the book *Two of Everything* by Lily Toy Hong. After reading, ask the kids what they would do if they had accidentally created a clone of themselves. Would they be happy? Scared? Worried? Would they play tricks on their friends, or would they leave the country? This kind of discussion will help fire up the children's imaginations for your brainstorming session.

Brainstorming (Next Fifteen Minutes)

Using a whiteboard or flip chart, make a chart for the kids to fill in by brainstorming. Draw two vertical lines and label the resulting columns Object, Best Case Scenario, and Worst Case Scenario, like this:

Object	Best Case Scenario	Worst Case Scenario

Ask the kids what they would put in a magic pot if they had one. Then help them tease out what the consequences of each choice would be. Whom would it benefit? Whom would it hurt? If you multiplied an ice cream cone enough times over, would you be able to throw your friends the biggest ice cream party ever and get a mention in the *Guinness World Records*? Would you keep throwing ice cream parties until all the local ice cream stores are put out of business and Earth's temperature goes down one and a half degrees? Would you accidentally set off a new Ice Age?

Hong neglects to mention how the old couple manages to keep their magic pot hidden from all the other people who would surely try to take it from them. After all, you wouldn't want your magic pot falling into the hands of an evil villain who wants to make *poisoned* ice cream, would you? (Put this in the Worst Case Scenario column.) As a precaution against evil villains, kids could consider what they would do to make sure that no one else finds out they have a magic pot. Write their suggestions on the board or flip chart on a new page or section.

Writing (Next Thirty Minutes)

Now the children have a premise and some different problems worth exploring. Ask the kids to find a seat at the tables, and pass out the handouts (or books, which can be downloaded from our website). Encourage the kids to write a story about the magic pot in any setting that they would like—it doesn't have to be set in a Chinese village. Kids will take a few of the items from the list and write about how duplicating those items worked out for their characters. Were the results good or bad? Kids should try to write a conclusion that shows the character faced with a problem or a potential problem and solving it.

Storytime (Last Ten Minutes)

Have the kids sit back down on the floor and take turns reading their stories from the same chair you used earlier. Applaud them, and listen for instances in their stories that reveal imagination and logical thinking. Say things like, "Wow, I really loved the way you explored how bewildered your dog would be if you cloned him! Great character development and plotting!" Kids learn from our praise of their work and their peers' work.

TITLE: _____

BY: _____

Setup: How did you get your magic pot? How did you find out that it doubles everything you put in it?

_____

_____

_____

Problem: What did you put in the pot? Why? What was the result? Did any of those things make trouble?

_____

_____

_____

Resolution: What did you do with the pot in the end? Sell it? Give it away? Keep it a secret? Break it?

_____

_____

_____

TRICKSTER TALES

FEATURED BOOK

***The Leopard's Drum,
An Asante Tale from West Africa***
by Jessica Souhami

Length: About one and a half hours

PR Blurb

After reading *The Leopard's Drum, An Asante Tale from West Africa* by Jessica Souhami, kids will analyze what makes trickster tales so satisfying and prominent in numerous cultures. Then kids will discuss what they value and write a trickster tale to reinforce those values. (**CCSS.ELA-LITERACY.RL.2.5, CCSS.ELA-LITERACY.RL.2.2, CCSS.ELA-LITERACY.W.2.3, CCSS.ELA-LITERACY.L.2.1.E**)

In *The Leopard's Drum,* Jessica Souhami tells a West African story about a boastful leopard who refuses to share his precious drum with anyone and a jealous sky god who offers a reward to any animal that can take the drum from the leopard and teach him a lesson. One by one the animals try: the stealthy python is unable to steal the drum, and the powerful elephant retreats in fear. When the humble tortoise says she wants to give it a try, everyone laughs. But she manages to use the leopard's arrogance against him and tricks him into climbing inside the drum to prove that it is really bigger than anyone else's. Once he's in, she traps him and collects her reward from the sky god, asking for a shell to protect her from fierce and vengeful leopards.

Storytime (First Ten Minutes)

Have the kids sit on the floor and listen while you read *The Leopard's Drum*. After reading, ask the kids why the other animals were so unsuccessful at getting the leopard to part with his drum. Ask them what sorts of traits the leopard has that make him so fearful to other animals. Then ask the children what lesson the leopard has learned in the end. And is he the only animal who acted foolishly in this story? How about all the animals who thought that getting the drum was a matter of size and power—did they learn anything from the tortoise?

Brainstorming: Anthropomorphism (Next Ten Minutes)

Invite the kids to sit at the tables and then pass out the handouts. Talk about how sometimes in one culture's folktales an animal is represented as being wise or good and in another culture's tales the same animal is evil or a bully.

This reversal often happens in folktales involving wolves or coyotes—sometimes it's the Big Bad Wolf, other times it's the Clever Coyote. Sometimes the rabbit is the fool, as in "The Tortoise and the Hare"; other times, the rabbit is the trickster, as in the Brer Rabbit tales. Ask the kids to match the animals in the right-hand column of the worksheet with the human traits on the left. Then invite the children to share their worksheets with the group so that you can compare their matches. Maybe one child thought hippos could be kind while another child thought they could be proud. It all depends on what the children's experience is or what they have read about hippos in books. There are no wrong answers!

Brainstorming: Prized Possessions (Next Ten Minutes)

In the book, the leopard's prized possession is his large drum. Drums must have been valued by the West African people who told the story. Ask the kids, "If you were to rewrite this story today, what would be the leopard's prized possession?"

If this question is difficult, you can try the following prompts:

» "Have you ever bragged to someone that you had something that was the best or the biggest or the most beautiful or the coolest? Has anyone else ever bragged to you? What was the object?"
» "If *you* could have anything you wished for, what would it be? The biggest house? The coolest car?"
» "Which would you rather have: the biggest dog or the cutest dog?" (Kids love questions like this.)

Using a flip chart or whiteboard, list any valuable objects the kids can think of.

Now, next to each object name, ask the kids to help you list one adjective that makes that object so special. Use superlatives. Your board will start to look like this:

» Monster Truck—Most Powerful
» Bike—Fastest
» Pony—Prettiest

Discuss how these prized possessions and their owners' opinions of them could open up the owners to jealousy in other people and theft by a trickster character. This result doubles when the owner is a mean person. Even though the trick involves inevitable dishonesty, we often root for trickster characters because it is so satisfying to see a bully or a mean person brought low.

Brainstorming: Plot (Next Ten Minutes)

Now try to expand the list to include ways that a trickster like the tortoise might be able to steal or win that prized possession away from the leopard.

The leopard prized his drum for being the biggest, and the tortoise must have seen that the drum looked big enough to trap the leopard inside. She just had to use reverse psychology to get him to lower his guard and try something stupid like crawling into his drum to prove how big it is.

Ask the kids how they could use reverse psychology and cunning to trick someone out of the prized possessions they listed by using the characteristics that make those possessions so special. In the case of a monster truck, for example, the trickster could lure the owner into driving it over something that just *happens* to be sitting on quicksand. Oops! Or in the case of the pretty pony, perhaps the trickster could tell the owner that he should cover her up so that no one will steal her and then help the owner hide her from himself! See what the kids come up with. Help them generate at least three ideas. Remember the following common tricks found in trickster tales:

> » Telling the fool that his prized object is not really that great so that he is infuriated and does something stupid in an attempt to prove how great it is (*The Leopard's Drum*)
> » Telling the fool that she should safeguard her special object and then convincing her that she should trust no one but the trickster (*The Little Mouse, the Red Ripe Strawberry, and the Big Hungry Bear* by Don and Audrey Wood)
> » Distracting the fool and luring him into a dangerous place (*Hansel and Gretel*; *Flossie and the Fox* by Patricia McKissack and Rachel Isadora)
> » Telling the fool that the trickster's worthless thing or undesirable state is better than hers so that she trades with the trickster and loses her more desirable thing or state (*Anansi Finds a Fool* by Verna Aardema and illustrated by Bryna Waldman; *Tom Sawyer* by Mark Twain)

Writing (Next Thirty Minutes)

For this activity I recommend asking the kids to pair up at the tables—this is a complex writing prompt, and kids will benefit from talking out ideas with a partner. Using all the brainstorming the children have done as a class, encourage them to work together to write their own unique retellings of *The Leopard's Drum* with whatever animal characters they want and whatever special objects they want to put in the story. Give the kids copies of the handouts or the books, which can be downloaded from our website.

Storytime (Last Ten Minutes)

Set out two storyteller's chairs and have all the kids sit on the floor. Invite the children to share the stories that they created with their partners. They can take turns reading the pages, or they can select someone who will read. Focus on praising them for the ideas they came up with. If they created a character who is a bully and the trickster puts him in his place, applaud them for their character development and satisfying ending!

YOUR NAME _____

For each personality trait on the left, draw a line to an animal on the right that you believe matches that trait. There are no wrong answers!

TRAIT	ANIMAL
Smart	Hippo
Rude	Rhino
Kind	Rabbit
Good Listener	Lion
Foolish	Mouse
Mean	Rat
Selfish	Bear
Proud	Snake
Careless	Dog
Hardworking	Cat
Friendly	Wolf
Shy	Bumblebee
Clumsy	Flamingo
Polite	Tiger
Whiny	Peacock
Annoying	Lizard
Sneaky	Frog

TITLE: _____

BY: _____

Setup: Who is the trickster? Who is the fool? What is it the fool loves more than anything?

_____

_____

_____

Problem: Is the fool who is being tricked a nice person or a mean person?

_____

_____

_____

Resolution: How does your trickster trick the fool? Does the fool learn a lesson?

_____

_____

_____

SMALL ACTORS FOLKTALE THEATER

FEATURED BOOK	ALTERNATE BOOK
Don't Leave an Elephant to Go and Chase a Bird by James Berry, illustrated by Ann Grifalconi	***Only One Cowry*** by Phillis Gershator, illustrated by David Soman

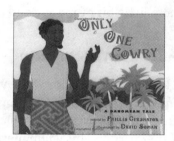

Length: About one and a half hours

Supplies

 » Name tags
 » Various office items as props

PR Blurb

It is said that "there are no small parts, only small actors." In this activity, every child in the group will be both a playwright and an actor, writing and performing a role in a play based on the African folktale *Don't Leave an Elephant to Go and Chase a Bird,* written by James Berry and illustrated by Ann Grifalconi. Parents are invited to come for the last fifteen minutes to be our audience! (**CCSS.ELA-LITERACY.W.2.3, CCSS.ELA-LITERACY.RL.2.2, CCSS. ELA-LITERACY.RL.2.5, CCSS.ELA-LITERACY.RL.2.6**)

In the folktale *Don't Leave an Elephant to Go and Chase a Bird* written by James Berry and illustrated by Ann Grifalconi, Anansi the Spiderman greets the sky god and receives a corncob out of thin air as a gift. Anansi gives the corncob to a hungry washerwoman, who gives him a gourd of water. He gives the gourd to a family of thirsty farmers, and they give him a yam. He walks all through the countryside making trades and bringing good things to people in need. He even gets a child whose mother can't feed him and then gives the child to a lonely, better-off woman. But when he makes the biggest win of all and gains a baby elephant, he gets distracted by a bird and the elephant runs away. His story was told among the West African people, who brought it to the Caribbean islands, to warn people about letting go of something valuable to chase after something else.

James Berry's book is out of print, but it's a classic that many libraries still carry. If you don't have it, there are other tales that follow the same structure of a series of trades from something small to something big. The Dahomean tale *Only One Cowry,* written by Phillis Gershator and illustrated by David Soman, is another African story that will work for this activity. In it a bright young man named Yo promises a king that he can find the king a bride with just one cowry shell as payment. He makes many trades that eventually make him and his whole village richer, and he succeeds in getting the king a nice bride. He shows that a little bit of money and a lot of effort can go a long way.

Storytime (First Ten Minutes)

Have the kids sit on the floor while you read either *Don't Leave an Elephant to Go and Chase a Bird* or *Only One Cowry.* If you have the book *Don't Leave an Elephant to Go and Chase a Bird,* you can have a discussion with the kids about Anansi's generosity and his willingness to use what little he has to help someone else in need. If you have the book *Only One Cowry,* you can talk about how the trades Yo makes with people are always mutually beneficial but result in Yo accumulating more and more wealth. Either way, talk about how, a long time ago, most people didn't carry money; they traded the things they had for the things they needed. Invite the kids to imagine what life would be like if we did away with all money and just traded goods and services. How would we know how valuable something was? How would we decide what to keep and what to trade?

Outlining Your Play (Next Fifteen Minutes)

Before your workshop, write the following list of items on your whiteboard or flip chart pad. (Thirty items are listed here, but you can list fewer if you have fewer than thirty kids.) You will want to gather these items in advance of the workshop, to be used as props in the play the kids will write. The items are easy to find around the library or classroom, or you can modify the list to fit what you have at hand.

- » Box of tissues
- » Water bottle
- » Flashlight
- » Popsicle stick
- » Sponge
- » Pencil
- » Rubber band
- » Book
- » Roll of tape
- » Cardboard box
- » Camera
- » Construction paper
- » Paint
- » White-out (correction fluid)
- » Soap
- » Paper towel
- » Band-Aid
- » Calculator
- » Ruler
- » Step stool
- » Chair
- » Scissors
- » Glue
- » Phone charger
- » Sticker
- » Bookmark
- » Paperweight
- » Pencil sharpener
- » Magnifying glass
- » Hand sanitizer

Show the kids your list and ask them which of these items they think is the most valuable. (Try to act shocked when they don't say, "The book!") Next to that item, write "30" (or the total number of items).

Ask the kids which item is the least valuable. Take a vote if you need to. Put a "1" next to that least valuable item. Now you can rank the remaining items from least to most valuable. Soon your list will start to look something like this:

» Rubber band—1
» Calculator—6
» Roll of tape—3
» Book—5

» Camera—7
» Band-Aid—4
» White-out—2

Writing (Next Thirty Minutes)

Tell the kids that they are going to write a play now for which they will all be the playwrights and the actors. Their play will be about a person who starts out with something very cheap and makes a bunch of trades to gain something valuable in the end. In order for this play to work, the children will need to think creatively and write a few lines from a character's point of view to show what item that character has and what item the character needs. Encourage the kids to add a level of magic to each item so that it is elevated from a boring pencil to a "magic pencil that will draw a friend" or a "special pencil that never runs out of lead."

Before the workshop, print as many copies of the handout as necessary, and number them. Each handout will be numbered differently. One handout will be numbered 1 for "What I need" and 2 for "What I have." The next handout will have numbers 2 and 3, and the next, numbers 3 and 4. You have to do the printing and numbering in advance so that you can easily pass out the handouts and props to the kids.

Pass out name tags with numbers 1 through 30 (or the total number of children in your group) written on them. Each child's handout will indicate which number you assign to that child, as well as the child's order of appearance in the play!

The kids will now write down the names of the items that correspond to the numbers they see on their handouts. For example, the child who got the handout numbered 1 and 2 will fill in the blanks so that the handout reads as follows:

» What I need: Rubber band (1)
» What I have: White-out (2)

The child who got the handout numbered 2 and 3 will write responses this way:

» What I need: White-out (2)
» What I have: Roll of tape (3)

Have the children answer the questions on the handout and write the "script" at the bottom. Encourage the kids to be creative. Maybe a character is fixing a broken spaceship, for which she needs the roll of tape. And she doesn't need her phone charger anymore because she's traveling to outer space. The kids can write anything they want and then write the action that they will do and the words that they will say. If you have a photocopier handy, you can photocopy the sheets so that the person playing Teacher (if it isn't you) can read his lines and the child who wrote the lines can read them, too. But if you are playing Teacher, you may not find this necessary. You're going to repeat the same thing again and again until the end.

Dress Rehearsal (Next Fifteen Minutes)

Set the props out on a table and ask the kids to take only the prop that their handout says they should have. You will take the item that you wrote a number 1 next to on the board (in this example, you will take the rubber band).

Do a run-through of your play, in which you play the role of Teacher inspired by the characters Anansi and Yo. Approach the child wearing the number 1 on his name tag and ask what he is doing. When he tells you why he is doing that and what he needs (a rubber band), you will say, "Well, well! It's your lucky day! It just so happens I have a rubber band." Offer him the rubber band (item number 1), for which he will thank you and repay you with the white-out (item number 2).

Then go to child 2, and ask what she is doing. She will say she needs white-out, and you will say, "Well, well! It's your lucky day! It just so happens I have white-out." Offer her the white-out (item number 2). She will thank you and repay you with the roll of tape (item number 3).

After all the kids have acted out their parts, and you end up with the camera (item number 30), end the play with this final line:

> "Wow! I started out with nothing but a rubber band and ended up with a camera. I guess it's my lucky day!"

Perform Your Play (Last Fifteen Minutes)

Have the kids put all their items back on the table where they got them. Then they can take the original item their character is supposed to start off with.

Invite the parents to come back in and watch your play! Tell the parents that you have worked together as a whole class to retell an African folktale about trading things and finding surprising value in them. Introduce the book you used. Be sure to mention that all the children wrote their own roles and added dialogue to the script. Then perform your play, and remember to end with those satisfying last words:

> "I guess it's my lucky day!"

What I Need: _____ (   ) ←Wear this number on your name tag

What I Have: _____ (   )

Answer the following questions about your character.
Why do you need what you need? What is it used for?

_____

_____

Why have you got the thing you already have? How might it be useful to someone else? Is there anything magical or special about it?

_____

_____

What will you do while you're on stage? How will you show how your life would be easier if only you had the thing you need?

_____

_____

- ✂

Write a script for you and your teacher to act out.

Teacher walks up to me and sees me _____ .

Teacher: Why are you _____ ?

Me: I wish I had _____ !

If I had it, I would _____ .

Teacher: Well, well! It's your lucky day! It just so happens I have _____ .
Here, take it. It's yours.

Me: You are so kind! Here, I have _____ .

It is very special. You can use it to _____ .
Please, take it!

Teacher: Thank you! You are very kind, too!

Animal Muses

Animals abound in stories for children, and it's not hard to see why. The many fascinating physical characteristics and behaviors of animals give artists a cornucopia of ideas for developing characters. Children's fascination with animals makes them a fun vehicle for telling stories, even stories that don't have anything in particular to do with animals. They also make it possible for children to explore deeper human feelings or to poke fun at a human trait without having to make fun of a human being. Children at this age are still learning to shift their points of view and appreciate another person's perspective, but they can easily develop stories about nonhuman characters whose feelings and opinions are more open to conjecture.[1]

CRAFT AND CHARACTER

During most of the lessons in this chapter, children will be learning how to jump into another creature's head and write convincing characters with unique perspectives. They will write diaries from the point of view of an animal to open a window into that animal's habitat and daily routine. They will learn about literary devices such as conceit and hyperbole. They will develop their informational and how-to writing skills. Children will also continue to hone their argumentative writing skills, brainstorming all the possible ways to persuade the reader of their opinions.

COMMON CORE STANDARDS

CCSS.ELA-LITERACY.L.2.1.E: Use adjectives and adverbs, and choose between them depending on what is to be modified.

CCSS.ELA-LITERACY.L.2.3.A: Compare formal and informal uses of English.

CCSS.ELA-LITERACY.L.2.4.D: Use knowledge of the meaning of individual words to predict the meaning of compound words (e.g., *birdhouse, lighthouse, housefly; bookshelf, notebook, bookmark*).

CCSS.ELA-LITERACY.L.2.5.A: Identify real-life connections between words and their use (e.g., *describe foods that are spicy or juicy*).

CCSS.ELA-LITERACY.L.2.5.B: Distinguish shades of meaning among closely related verbs (e.g., *toss, throw, hurl*) and closely related adjectives (e.g., *thin, slender, skinny, scrawny*).

CCSS.ELA-LITERACY.W.2.2: Write informative/explanatory texts in which they introduce a topic, use facts and definitions to develop points, and provide a concluding statement or section.

CCSS.ELA-LITERACY.W.2.3: Write narratives in which they recount a well-elaborated event or short sequence of events, include details to describe actions, thoughts, and feelings, use temporal words to signal event order, and provide a sense of closure.

CCSS.ELA-LITERACY.W.2.5: With guidance and support from adults and peers, focus on a topic and strengthen writing as needed by revising and editing.

CCSS.ELA-LITERACY.RL.2.3: Describe how characters in a story respond to major events and challenges.

CCSS.ELA-LITERACY.RL.2.6: Acknowledge differences in the points of view of characters, including by speaking in a different voice for each character when reading dialogue aloud.

CCSS.ELA-LITERACY.RI.2.5: Know and use various text features (e.g., captions, bold print, subheadings, glossaries, indexes, electronic menus, icons) to locate key facts or information in a text efficiently.

IF I HAD A DINOSAUR

FEATURED BOOK

If I Had a Raptor
by George O'Connor

Length: About one hour and fifteen minutes

Supplies

Additional books on prehistoric and mythical animals

PR Blurb

After reading *If I Had a Raptor* by George O'Connor, kids will make an argument for getting an unusual pet. They will take the characteristics of a typical house pet to brainstorm all the reasons why an unusual pet, like a dinosaur, would or wouldn't make a good home companion. (**CCSS.ELA-LITERACY.W.2.2, CCSS.ELA-LITEACY.W.2.5, CCSS.ELA-LITERACY.RI.2.5, CCSS.ELA-LITERACY.L.2.3.A**)

One of the things that always struck me about George O'Connor's book *If I Had a Raptor* was the ways in which the little girl in the story expects her wished-for pet velociraptor to act like a cat. The unnamed narrator is convinced that she would find a raptor willing to snuggle on her lap and eat from a bowl on the floor. She even contemplates how the raptor would tell her whether she is hungry or not, walking away from her food bowl with her tail held high when she's not and staring things down with the intensity of a hunter when she is.

Obviously, this book is more imaginative than scientific. Kids who are obsessed with learning facts about dinosaurs will be eager to point that out. In fact, O'Connor fully intended to write this dinosaur book about . . . a cat! During a reading, O'Connor told his audience, "My cat, in many ways, is like a dinosaur, so that's kind of what this book's about."[2]

Storytime (First Ten Minutes)

Read *If I Had a Raptor* and discuss whether the book is about a dinosaur or a cat. Ask questions while you read, such as, "Isn't a bell sort of undignified for a majestic creature like a dinosaur?" You can introduce the discussion like this: "You know, every time I read this book I wonder, shouldn't someone tell the narrator that she can really get all the things she wants from a cat? And then she wouldn't have to resurrect an extinct prehistoric animal." Ask the kids if they have pets and if they see any similarities between their pets and O'Connor's raptor.

Brainstorming (Next Ten Minutes) ·····································

Ask the kids to name some animals that are not currently available to own as pets. They can be real or fantastical—panda bears and unicorns, they're all game. Kids can even make up a new animal completely, as long as they can describe its characteristics to the group. Write the animals on the board or flip chart, and ask the kids to help you list at least two or three reasons why each one is not a pet their parents would ever bring home.

Now ask the kids if there is any compromise they could make with their parents so that they could get that animal for a pet. Perhaps there is some adaptation that would make the pet more house-friendly. In the book, the little girl puts a bell on her velociraptor so that she can find the animal. In the end of the story, the bell saves the little girl from becoming the raptor's lunch. Ask the kids how they would solve the problem of why that animal is usually undesirable as a pet.

Mini-Lesson on Persuasive Writing and Knowing Your Audience (Next Ten Minutes) ·····································

Ask the kids if they can spot any instances of ethos, logos, and pathos. (Review these concepts discussed at length in lesson 4.) An example of logos (facts) would be the narrator's claim that velociraptors would have special eyes for seeing at night. (Kids might be interested to know that raptors really were nocturnal, according to paleontologists who study the scleral rings and eye sockets in raptor skulls! You may want to put a few books about raptors on display for kids to learn more.)

Ask the kids who they think is the audience for this book. Is this book written to convince a parent to buy a raptor for his daughter? Or is it written to convince a child how delightful it would be to own a raptor? Does the narrator value facts or emotional enthusiasm? Is her argument strong or weak?

Write the following sentences on the board. Ask the children which sentence appeals to them more.

> » A velociraptor would be an easy pet because it would sleep all day, and it would fit in the house because it's hardly bigger than a cat.
> » A velociraptor would be the cutest pet ever with its fluffy little feathers!

Now try to rethink this book with the goal of persuading a parent to buy one. What do parents value? Remind the children to think about their audience. Ask the kids if they have ever tried to convince their parents of something. Did their parents prefer facts (logos) or emotional appeals (pathos)? Would their parents be more open to the idea of a raptor pet if the children told them that they would come to love it as a member of the family? Or would they be more open to it if the children explained that the raptor wouldn't be as messy as a dog because it wouldn't shed any fur? Maybe either argument would be valid depending on who the children's parents are—there's no wrong answer!

Research (Next Fifteen Minutes)

Let each child choose one of the books you put out about mythical creatures and prehistoric animals. Have the children sit at the tables and read about one animal, looking for at least three interesting facts about the animal. They will write these facts down on the worksheet provided. Show the kids how to find their desired animal from a table of contents or an index and how to find facts that way.

Writing (Next Twenty Minutes)

Tell the kids they are going to practice making an argument for why they really should have this pet. Remind them to consider their audience—in this case, adults who want to hear practical plans and facts. Move among the tables to help the kids generate their ideas.

Encourage the kids to anticipate how their arguments will be received by their parents. Their parents still may not want to get a dinosaur for a pet, but perhaps some compromise can be found. Instead of a woolly mammoth, maybe they could get a baby elephant, or instead of a saber-toothed tiger, maybe a kitten would meet their needs. The kids can use either the handouts or the books you can download from our website.

Storytime (Last Ten Minutes)

Have the kids all sit on the floor and then invite them one by one to read their arguments in the storyteller's chair. If they wrote an ending, great! Applaud them for that. And any facts they included will be great things to focus on praising.

IS YOUR ANIMAL REAL OR PRETEND? _____

Write down three things you learned about your animal:

_____

_____

_____

_____

Write down one silly fact about your animal. You can make something up!

_____

_____

Can you think of a real, living animal that is like your animal in some way? How?

_____

_____

Unusual Animals to Try

Woolly mammoth	Triceratops	Nuralagus rex
Unicorn	Stegosaurus	Glyptodon
Dragon	Tyrannosaurus	Megatherium
Pegasus	Ankylosaurus	Quetzalcoatlus
Mermaid	Iguanodon	Dire wolf
Saber-toothed tiger	Diplodocus	Paraceratherium
Giant sloth	Hadrosaur	Mastodon
Werewolf	Theropod	Woolly rhinoceros

IF I HAD A: _____

BY: _____

_____

_____

_____

_____

_____

_____

HOW TO THROW A UNICORN PARTY

FEATURED BOOK

Dragons Love Tacos
by Adam Rubin, illustrated by Daniel Salmieri

Length: About one and a half hours

PR Blurb

After reading *Dragons Love Tacos* by Adam Rubin and illustrated by Daniel Salmieri, kids create a how-to guide for throwing the best monster or mythical creature party. They will learn also about tone, voice, and question-and-answer formats common in informational how-to writing. (**CCSS.ELA-LITERACY.W.2.2, CSS.ELA-LITERACY.W.2.5, CCSS.ELA-LITERACY.L.2.3.A**)

Have you ever wondered how to get a dragon to like you? Of course, you have. I bet you didn't know it was as easy as throwing a taco party. Never thrown a taco party for dragons before? Well, Adam Rubin and Daniel Salmieri will turn you into a seasoned taco party host or hostess in no time. They'll share all the best secrets, from how many tacos to buy ("The best way to judge is to get a boat and fill the boat with tacos") to which pitfalls you need to avoid and how to do that ("In fact, bury the spicy salsa in the backyard"). And even if you never get a chance to put all this helpful dragon advice to use, the matter-of-fact but friendly tone and the whimsical illustrations make for wonderful reading every time.

Storytime (First Ten Minutes)

Have the kids sit on the floor and listen as you read *Dragons Love Tacos*. After reading, discuss the author's voice. Does the author sound like he knows what he is talking about? How does he convince you that he knows so much about dragons? Does he list a bunch of credentials and degrees? Or does he use sound bites that are both assertive and wise? ("[I]f you want to make friends with dragons, tacos are key.")

Does the author speak *formally* (as if he is addressing the Pope) or *informally* (as if you, the reader, are his close friend)? If the kids are not sure, point out the use of such phrases as "Oh boy" and "Hey, kid!"

If you have English language learners, ask them to help you demonstrate to the class how people convey formal and informal tones in their native languages. In Spanish, for example, kids would use "usted" to address an adult (formal) and "tú" to address a friend (informal). But in English, there is only one "you," so the difference is more subtle, depending heavily on the context of the sentence.

Mini-Lesson on the Basics of How-To Books (Next Fifteen Minutes)

Ask the kids if they have ever tried learning how to make or do something with only a book to guide them. Which would they rather have: a teacher who can help them troubleshoot problems that arise, or a book?

I'd be surprised if your students say they would prefer the book, because studies have shown that most people would prefer to have a teacher guide them through something they don't know how to do. Even when reading a book or viewing text on the Internet is more convenient, 78 percent of adult students would rather have a teacher right in front of them in a traditional classroom.[3] You can share this finding with the kids and ask them why they think it's true. How does it feel to learn something on your own, with no adult there to explain it another way if you aren't getting it? How does it feel to learn *anything* new—isn't it always a little scary? After all, there's a reason why they call it "stepping out of your *comfort* zone"!

For this reason, one of the most important staples of how-to writing is a friendly, conversational tone. If the students reflect on how uncomfortable it is to learn a new skill, they will be able to appreciate the importance of putting the reader at ease. When a writer adopts a friendly, informal tone, it's easier for the reader to feel as though she is connecting with a human being instead of just symbols printed on a page.

So how does a writer develop that friendly, conversational tone?

One way is by giving the reader a sense that a "conversation" is happening. The writer anticipates any questions the reader might ask (just as I did earlier). In *Dragons Love Tacos,* the author anticipates that the reader will probably want to know how many tacos to buy. The author asks the question, then follows up with a suggestion to fill a boat with tacos. It's almost as if the reader is having a conversation with the author and he is taking the questions right out of the reader's mouth.

Now review the book with the kids and ask if they can identify any other instances in which the author anticipates a question being asked, asks the question himself, and then gives the reader his answer. There are several others ("Why do dragons hate spicy salsa? Well, . . ." "Why do dragons love parties? Maybe it's the conversation.").

Brainstorming (Next Ten Minutes)

Before class, put a list of mythical or extinct creatures on the whiteboard or flip chart pad. You can use these:

» Unicorns	» Yetis	» Centaurs
» Trolls	» Leprechauns	» Satyrs
» Fairies	» Santa's elves	» Elves
» Woolly mammoths	» Dinosaurs	

Mythical or extinct creatures work for this exercise because their preferences are not well known. (You might have to explain a few of the names to the kids. Better yet, print out pictures from the Internet or photocopy pictures from books!) Then invite the kids to help you fill in that list with things those animals might like. Maybe unicorns love balloons, or trolls love doing the limbo. Maybe leprechauns love finger painting, or centaurs love basketball. To help out, you could list random foods, games, and activities that the kids can choose from.

Rewriting and Revising (Next Ten Minutes)

Pick one of those pairings of a creature and a food or a plaything, and write a simple sentence about it, like this:

> *You will need a really big helium tank for your unicorn party because unicorns like really big balloons.*

Now ask the kids to help you rewrite that sentence with more pizzazz. "Really big" is not very descriptive. *How* big? Bigger than a piano? Bigger than a car? Once you've got a few ideas for how to describe the size of the balloons, the kids' imaginations should be revved up to start writing their own how-to manuals for throwing a mythical creature party.

Ask the kids what kinds of disasters might befall that party. Might the unicorns' horns be too sharp and pop all the balloons? What if you put marshmallows on the tips of their horns? Would that fix it?

Pre-writing (Next Ten Minutes)

Have the kids sit at the tables and then pass out the pre-writing worksheets. These worksheets will help the kids get started on their stories.

Writing (Next Twenty Minutes)

Pass out the handouts or books that you can download from our website. Encourage the kids to write as though they are talking to a friend, assuring him that his efforts to befriend a centaur will be successful as long as he follows some simple steps. Of course, those steps will probably be anything but simple—encourage the kids to think big and get crazy with their stories!

Storytime (Last Ten Minutes)

Now ask the kids to return to the floor and invite them to share their stories one by one in the storyteller's chair. Applaud the kids for things like using a friendly tone, or giving great examples, or imagining hilarious consequences. Focus on the positive, and leave things like spelling and grammar for another day.

Your name: _____

Your creature: _____

Where does your creature live? _____

What does your creature like to eat? _____

What does your creature like to do? _____

Is there any reason your reader might be scared of this creature?

_____

SAMPLE QUESTIONS

Pick one of these questions:

So you want to make friends with a _____ ?

Where do you find a _____ , anyway?

How will you know your _____ is happy?

Have you ever spoken to a _____ before?

Now write an answer to that question:

_____

_____

_____

_____

HOW TO MAKE FRIENDS WITH A: _____

BY: _____

_____

_____

_____

_____

MY PUPPY BROTHER

FEATURED BOOK	ALTERNATE BOOK

My Father the Dog
by Elizabeth Bluemle,
illustrated by Randy Cecil

My Teacher Is a Monster!
by Peter Brown

Length: About one hour

PR Blurb

After reading *My Father the Dog* by Elizabeth Bluemle and illustrated by Randy Cecil, kids will write a silly argument (in a serious tone) comparing people to animals while learning to use a literary device called *conceit*. (**CCSS.ELA-LITERACY.W.2.2, CCSS.ELA-LITERACY.L.2.3.A, CCSS.ELA-LITERACY.L.2.1.E, CCSS.ELA-LITERACY.L.2.5.B**)

My Father the Dog by Elizabeth Bluemle and illustrated by Randy Cecil makes a very clear and irrefutable argument for the speaker's conviction that her father is merely "pretending" to be a human. She knows he is really a dog because he acts like one, and she doesn't shy away from giving us specific evidence to back up that claim—even when it involves pit stops on trees and innocent looks after passing gas. There is no fooling this little girl that her loyal, lovable dad is a dog, but she's willing to humor him—after all, her mom says he can stay.

If your library does not own *My Father the Dog,* you could use the more recent book *My Teacher Is a Monster* by Peter Brown. The boy in this book starts by presenting all his evidence proving that his teacher must be a monster because she is so mean, but his impression of her softens one day when he bumps into her at the park.

Storytime (First Ten Minutes)

Have the kids sit on the floor while you read *My Father the Dog.* When you're finished, ask them if the narrator made a strong argument. Did she present enough evidence? Did the pictures show the similarities well enough? Can the kids think of anything else dogs do that people do as well?

Brainstorming and Mini-Lesson on Conceit (Next Ten Minutes)

Ask the kids if they can help you count the number of different reasons the narrator gives for comparing her dad to a dog. Tally the reasons on the board or flip chart. (I counted seventeen, but I could have missed one—how many do you count?)

Explain to the kids that when a writer presents that many arguments for making a strange comparison such as a human father to a dog, the writer has developed a literary device known as a *conceit*. A conceit is an extended metaphor that uses many metaphors or similes to make a comparison between two things that would not normally be compared.

Seventeen reasons why a father is like a dog may seem like a lot, but ask the kids if they can try their hand at coming up with a smaller number, say, three reasons.

Ask the children what their favorite animals are. Write a few down on separate areas of your board or separate pages of your flip chart.

For each one, invite the kids to come up with at least three similarities between the animal and a person. It could be a specific person they know or just people in general. This exercise will be especially easy if the person is a baby. (I am always finding similarities between babies and animals—their total innocence and lack of worry about people's opinions or judgment remind us that we are all members of the same animal kingdom!)

Your list might start to take shape like this:

» Puppies and babies both drool.
» Puppies and babies both howl when they're sad.
» Puppies and babies both stick their tongues out all the time.
» Puppies and babies will both wake you up at night.

If the kids have any trouble coming up with similarities, remind them that all animals (humans included) communicate. Body language is most of our communication, right? What kinds of body language do animals display? What kinds of sounds do they make?

You can even turn to other animal processes like poop and gas—because those kinds of things were included in Bluemle's book, after all. I never restrict kids from writing about farts and poop. I always figure, if they are at a library program to do some creative writing, they have already written all day in school, and they are here to have *fun*. And who am I to say that farts aren't an appropriate subject for literature? Writing about underpants certainly worked out for Dav Pilkey!

Additional Literary Influences You Can Mention (Next Five Minutes)

There are a lot of children's books in which older siblings characterize their baby siblings as animals. In *Junie B. Jones and a Little Monkey Business* by Barbara Park, Junie learns that her new baby brother is a "cute little monkey" and immediately starts thinking of all the ways she could cash in on this amazing monkey brother. Everybody wants to be the first to see her "monkey," and she's not afraid to make a profit from showing him off!

In *The Talented Clementine* by Sara Pennypacker, Clementine's toddler brother goes wild whenever she sings Elvis Presley's "Hound Dog"—so much so that she considers working him into her act in the upcoming talent show. She plans to have him wear a leash and get on all fours barking while she sings the song. Unfortunately, her parents step in and put a stop to it the moment she mentions the leash she plans to make him wear.

Writing (Next Twenty Minutes)

Have the kids sit at the tables and then pass out the worksheet or books that you can download from our website. Explain that the children need to make a strong, well-reasoned argument for why this person is really a puppy or a cat or an alien. Well-reasoned arguments should be backed up by evidence, so in this exercise the children will need to write at least four examples of "evidence" of their claim.

Encourage the kids to use a "formal" tone in their arguments. When Elizabeth Bluemle's narrator says, "Consider the evidence," the sophisticated language makes her sound like a lawyer, and it makes us take her seriously. So no matter how silly the kids' comparisons are, remind them to present their arguments with a serious *tone*. That will make the result even more hysterical.

Encourage the kids also to include some sort of concluding statement. It can be a statement about how much they love that person, or how much fun that person is because of all his quirks.

Storytime (Last Ten Minutes)

Ask the kids to return to their seats on the floor and then invite them to come one by one to the storyteller's chair where you read *My Father the Dog*. As they read their own arguments comparing people to animals, praise them for making interesting connections, arguing their point persuasively, and using a formal, serious voice.

TITLE: _____

BY: _____

_____ may look like a human, but don't be fooled!

_____ is really a _____ !

Evidence:

1. _____

_____

2. _____

_____

3. _____

_____

4. _____

_____

TAKE YOUR POEM FOR A WALK

FEATURED BOOK	ALTERNATE BOOK

Meow Ruff:
A Story in Concrete Poetry
by Joyce Sidman,
illustrated by Michelle Berg

A Poke in the I: A Collection
of Concrete Poems selected
by Paul B. Janeczko,
illustrated by Chris Raschka

Length: About one hour

PR Blurb

After reading some poems from *Meow Ruff: A Story in Concrete Poetry* by Joyce Sidman and illustrated by Michelle Berg, kids will write concrete poems about animals with words written in the shapes of their animal characters. (**CCSS. ELA-LITERACY.L.2.4.D, CCSS.ELA-LITERACY.L.2.5.A, CCSS.ELA-LITERACY.L.2.5.B, CCSS.ELA-LITERACY.L.2.1.E**)

Almost everything in *Meow Ruff: A Story in Concrete Poetry,* written by Joyce Sidman and illustrated by Michelle Berg, is made up of printed words. The grass is a poem; the tree is a poem; the clouds are a poem with a scrumptious-sounding kenning worthy of the pastry-loving Norse people who gave us that poetic form: "sugary white sky-muffin" (yum!). The puppy and cat, which are the protagonists in this story, start out fearful of each other in their word arcs that indicate their speech. But a change in the weather forces them both into the same hiding place, and they learn to like each other. I love the way the poems about nature change very gradually, the way that clouds change shape slowly in the wind. The poems become more active, going from mostly descriptions to mostly verbs. Although this isn't so much a book that can be read aloud in one sitting, it offers many delights for more extended and careful readings.

If you have time, I recommend also reading and sharing the book *A Poke in the I: A Collection of Concrete Poems* selected by Paul B. Janeczko and illustrated by Chris Raschka. It will be an excellent alternative for this activity. It offers kids many different takes on the concept of a concrete poem, from the poem about a popsicle shaped like a popsicle to the poem about acrobats in which the word *acrobat* can be read in many directions as though it is doing flips in the air. There's a poem about tennis that has to be read by going rapidly back and forth from one side to the other, and the titular poem about needing contact lenses "like I need a poke in the eye" is written in the form of a vision test chart.

Storytime (First Ten Minutes)

Have the kids sit on the floor to hear poems from *Meow Ruff: A Story in Concrete Poetry* (or *A Poke in the I* if that book is more available to you). You won't be able to read the entire book to the kids, but you could select a few poems that move you and share those. I usually share two of the tree poems and some of the cloud poems. At least once I will ask the kids to close their eyes so that they can let the words wash over them and focus more on the sounds of the words than on the pictures.

Brainstorming (Next Ten Minutes)

Have the kids take a seat at the tables, and pass out a blank sheet of paper to each child. Ask the children to write the name of an animal at the top of the paper. Beneath the name, they will write down images, characteristics, behaviors—*anything* they can think of pertaining to that animal. Encourage them to get as many ideas down on paper as they can in five minutes.

Now ask them to think of ways that they could shape their words to look like the animal they are writing about. Ask questions such as these:

» What should the animal be doing in the picture? Sitting still? Playing?
» What direction should the words go in? Will it be horizontal and left to right, like the grass in *Meow Ruff*? Or vertical, like the raindrops falling? (There are many great examples of multidirectional print in *A Poke in the I*, too.)
» Will you use big letters, little letters, or a combination of the two?

Writing (Next Twenty Minutes)

Pass out the "picture frame" handouts and provide markers and crayons for kids who want to write their poems in color. Kids will write their names on the line at the top and create their concrete poem inside the frame. Tell the kids that they will be guessing each other's animals, so encourage them to try to make it hard to guess! This strategy will drive them to write more metaphorically!

Storytime (Last Fifteen Minutes)

Invite the children one by one to sit in the storyteller's chair and read their concrete poem. Then ask the group if they can guess what animal it is. The reveal will be when the child turns the page around and shows the group what the concrete poem looks like.

Compliment the children on their use of imagery, details, metaphorical and figurative language, and the shaping of the words.

OPTIONAL EXERCISE FOR ADVANCED YOUNG WRITERS

If you have any kids who are eager for a challenge, and provided you have time, you can teach them how to write a kenning.

Kennings are a wonderful form of poetic language for children to try, because they resemble riddles! The kenning, which originated in Norse and Anglo-Saxon literature, takes a simple, common noun and replaces it with two different (and sometimes odd-looking) nouns joined together. "Whale-road" (meaning the ocean) is one of the most famous Old English kennings, found in *Beowulf*. "Ring-giver" or "gold-giver" is another common one, as is "corpse-maker."

Here are some kennings that children might be more familiar with:

- Couch potato
- Rug rat
- Bookworm

When helping children write something new, always try to root it in something they have already written or expressed during pre-writing. Look at the words the child wrote down while brainstorming. If she is writing about a dog and has written

- wags its tail
- smiles with long, wet tongue hanging out

then she could convert those descriptions to kennings like this:

- tail-wagger
- tongue-dangler

A POEM BY

_____

DON'T SWEAT THE SNOW STUFF
Self-Help for Stressed Penguins

FEATURED BOOK	ALTERNATE BOOK

FEATURED BOOK

Penguin Problems
by Jory John,
illustrated by Lane Smith

Length: About one and a half hours

ALTERNATE BOOK

***Don't Sweat the Small Stuff . . .
And It's All Small Stuff***
by Richard Carlson

PR Blurb

After reading *Penguin Problems* by Jory John and illustrated by Lane Smith and a selection from *Don't Sweat the Small Stuff . . . And It's All Small Stuff* by Richard Carlson, kids will do a thought experiment moving the penguin to a place without those challenges but keeping his gloomy character the same. Then they will write a self-help text for an animal of their choice to teach it some coping skills. (**CCSS.ELA-LITERACY.W.2.2, CCSS.ELA-LITERACY.W.2.5, CCSS.ELA-LITERACY.RL.2.3, CCSS.ELA-LITERACY.RL.2.6, CCSS.ELA-LITERACY.L.2.3.A**)

Despite the fact that penguins are considered by many kids I know to be among the most *adorable* animals on the planet, the little penguin in *Penguin Problems* by Jory John and illustrated by Lane Smith finds absolutely no joy in his existence. He gripes about the weather, the water, the dark nights, and the blinding sunlight on the snow. He gripes about the leopard seals, sharks, and orcas that all want to eat him. He feels totally alone in his problems—especially the problem of looking "the same as everybody else." This causes him to work himself up to a full-blown tantrum, shouting that "nobody even cares!" Eventually, a walrus overhears him complaining and makes a gallant effort to enlighten Penguin that everyone has problems but that there is still much to appreciate in life. The lecture fails to bring about its intended result, and Penguin gripes some more, wondering "what does a walrus know about penguin problems?" (Penguin has a point, you know. What is a walrus even *doing* in Antarctica?)

Although they may not learn much about the penguin's habitat from this book, kids will learn an important truth of how silly it sounds when someone whines constantly about his problems—and how hard it is to break that habit. They will certainly see a little of themselves and their peers in Penguin and, being smarter than a penguin, will probably put the walrus's words to some use!

Storytime (First Ten Minutes)

Have the children sit on the floor and listen to you read *Penguin Problems*. After you read, ask the kids why they thought the walrus's lecture failed to persuade the penguin to think more positively. What if the walrus had approached the situation differently? Perhaps dumping that long lecture on somebody was only going to make the listener defensive. Is there another way that would have been more convincing?

Learn Persuasive Writing from *Don't Sweat the Small Stuff* (Next Fifteen Minutes)

Don't Sweat the Small Stuff . . . And It's All Small Stuff by Richard Carlson has sold millions of copies and has spawned a whole series of Don't Sweat books geared specifically to helping people at various stages of life. There is a Don't Sweat the Small Stuff book for moms, for families, for teens, at work . . . now all we need is a *Don't Sweat the Small Stuff . . . for Penguins!*

Read an excerpt from Carlson's book. For children I recommend the chapter "Allow Yourself to Be Bored." It's such good advice for young writers. Kids try to fill every minute of their lives with television, video games, YouTube, and other distractions. If they were a little more bored, they might spend more time learning, creating, and developing their minds!

Draw the kids' attention to the pronouns that the author uses in this chapter. You may want to give the kids an overview of pronouns (*I, you, he, she, we, they*) on the whiteboard or flip chart. The author spends a good deal of time in this chapter on "I" and "we" statements. He starts with statements such as "For many of us," and then moves into a story about himself. Then he spends some more time in the "we," with lines such as "While we're eating dinner, we wonder what's for dessert. While we're eating dessert, we ponder what we should do afterward." He talks about things that are *universal,* that anyone can relate to. (Put *universal* on the board—it's a good vocabulary term for this lesson.) He is careful not to address the reader as "you" until *after* he has established that he and the reader are one "we."

How is Carlson's writing different from the walrus's speech? Here are some things that I noticed:

» The walrus starts his lecture with "you" and then moves on to "we" and finishes with "I am certain that, when you think about it, you'll realize that you are exactly where you need to be."
» The walrus uses a lot of poetic language, while Carlson uses more commonplace examples like "dinner" and "dessert."

» The walrus sounds pedantic, and his tone is very formal, while the tone in *Don't Sweat the Small Stuff* is informal and nonjudgmental.

A Thought Experiment (Next Ten Minutes)

Ask the kids to imagine sending the penguin in Jory John and Lane Smith's book on vacation somewhere. Change his setting—*but not his character!* Ask the kids if they can think of a place that *doesn't* have whales, or snow, or other penguins. It shouldn't be hard. If they move him there, but leave his character the same, what will happen?

He will probably find other things to complain about. Maybe his thick plumage will leave him maladapted to the hot, humid air of a jungle. And maybe he won't encounter any seals or whales there, but what about jaguars? He'd be an easy lunch for them.

Doing this exercise will teach the kids another truth that Richard Carlson talks about in *Don't Sweat the Small Stuff*: that "wherever you go, there you are." You can never escape from yourself, so the best thing you can do is change your attitude.

Brainstorming (Next Fifteen Minutes)

Ask the kids to suggest an animal that has problems. With their participation, try to fill the whiteboard or flip chart pad with a list of all those problems—from who is hunting him to what the climate is where he lives to what food choices he has and anything else they come up with. Be careful to always write whatever they say, even if you don't agree with it at first. Give everybody the feeling that they are contributing to the creative discussion.

Now ask the kids if there is anything about that animal's experience that they can empathize with. Do *they* ever resent having to eat the same food week after week? Do they ever resent cold or rainy weather? Is it normal to feel irritated by things like that? Of course it is!

Ask the kids to think of the last time they were irritated by the weather. Maybe a long-awaited baseball game had to be canceled because of rain. Or maybe a picnic was ruined by a sudden thunderstorm that was nowhere in the weather forecast. What did they do to cope? Did they find other things to do, with family and friends who were just as compelled to stay indoors as they were? Put their suggestions on the board or flip chart pad.

Writing (Next Twenty Minutes)

Now that the kids have thought about the struggles that animals have and have developed empathy for those struggles, invite them to sit at the tables and use the handouts to write one page of a class book that will be a compendium of self-help advice for animals! Each child will choose an animal and put that animal's name on the line at the top so that, for example, the page will be titled "Don't Sweat the Small Stuff ... for Bears" if the child chose bears. You can then staple all the children's pages together into a book.

If you're working with English language learners, you can model some sentences for them on the whiteboard:

Do you ever get mad when _____?

I do. But it helps if I _____ .

I know it must be hard when _____ .

I'm sorry you have to deal with _____ .

Storytime (Last Ten Minutes)

Have the kids sit on the floor again and invite them to come one by one to read their pages of the self-help book to their peers from the storyteller's chair you sat in earlier. Compliment them on the ways that they put their empathy to use in writing advice for their chosen animal. Applaud them for their understanding of the animal's habitat or place in the food chain as well. Praise them for finding things that are universal and not just specific to that animal's condition.

Now if only those animals could read the kids' book and know that, somewhere, there is a human child who is sympathetic to their pain!

DON'T SWEAT THE SMALL STUFF . . . FOR _____

BY: _____

Draw a picture of your animal whining about something.

What would you say to help your animal?

_____

_____

_____

SELF-HELP FOR STRESSED ANIMALS

BY KIDS AT

_____
(your institution)

On: _____ (date)

Compiled by: _____ (teacher's name)

PUBLIC SERVICE ANNOUNCEMENT
Beware the Giant Humans

FEATURED BOOK	ALTERNATE BOOK

Little Mouse's Big Book of Beasts
by Emily Gravett

Little Mouse's Big Book of Fears
by Emily Gravett

Length: About one hour

PR Blurb

After reading *Little Mouse's Big Book of Beasts* by Emily Gravett, kids will revise a diagram about humans and rewrite it from the point of view of a small creature like a bug or a spider, gaining a fun perspective on how scary kids can be to the animals that frighten them. (**CCSS.ELA-LITERACY.W.2.2, CCSS.ELA-LITERACY.W.2.5, CCSS.ELA-LITERACY.RL.2.6, CCSS.ELA-LITERACY.RI.2.5, CCSS.ELA-LITERACY.L.2.1.E, CCSS.ELA-LITERACY.L.2.3.A**)

In *Little Mouse's Big Book of Beasts* by Emily Gravett, there are two different authorial voices. There's the voice of the author, Emily Gravett, who gives us verses about lions, sharks, crabs, owls, and bears. And there's the voice of Little Mouse, who complains that he does not like "LOUD lions or sharp-tempered sharks" and goes through the book redoing the illustrations so that he has some measure of power over these fierce animals. The book is full of Gravett's characteristic out-of-the-box illustrating style, with lots of flaps to flip and holes to peep through. Little Mouse proves to be an interesting character, one with heroism and humor. Just as he tacks silly high heels on the rhinoceros to prevent it from stomping on him, he is also willing to turn that same funny imagination around on himself, decking out the Mouse at the end with all manner of claws, talons, beaks, and jaws! Perhaps this is his dream for what he wishes to be, or perhaps he simply has a beef with Gravett, who is too quick to write off mice as "weak"—something our hero Little Mouse certainly is not!

Storytime (First Ten Minutes)

While the kids are seated on the floor, share with them *Little Mouse's Big Book of Beasts* by Emily Gravett. It's not a traditional read-aloud, and you might find it easiest either to skip some pages or skip the verses about each animal and just read Little Mouse's lines (written in watercolor). See if the kids can volunteer examples of the ways that Little Mouse gets the upper hand over these scary beasts with his creative changes to the illustrations. Ask them what's funny about each illustration and whether they think the book is better with or without Little Mouse's additions and revisions.

Brainstorming (Next Fifteen Minutes)

Using the whiteboard or flip chart, ask the kids to help you list some small animals that they find scary. Most people find spiders, bees, flies, roaches, and other insects and arachnids unpleasant. Make a list of at least ten small animals that the kids would go out of their way to avoid contact with.

Then ask them if they have ever heard it said of bees that "they are more afraid of you than you are of them." Is this true? Ask the kids to help you list all the reasons why a bee or fly might be afraid of a child like them. Ask them to jump inside the mind of a small insect and look at human beings from that perspective. You will start to get a list of traits like these:

- » Big
- » Fast
- » Unpredictable
- » Noisy
- » Stomping feet

Try to get a long list of examples, including the implements people use to attack pests.

Writing (Next Twenty Minutes)

Have the kids sit at the tables, and pass out the worksheets with the diagram of children. Tell the kids they are going to rewrite that diagram from the point of view of one of the small creatures they listed on the board earlier. Their challenge will be to change this cheery vocabulary diagram of human body parts into a "public service announcement" for bees or ants, warning against every aspect of humans that might be a threat to their survival. Should the boy's hand be called merely "hand," or should it be called "Evil Swatter That Sometimes Comes Armed with Spray Bottles"? Should the girl's shoe be called "shoe," or should it be called "Cruel Stomper That Can Crush You Flat"? If you have English language learners, give them the vocabulary list titled "Verbs That Would Scare a Small Animal" for some suggestions if they are struggling.

At the bottom of the worksheet, the children should draw the animal that is the author of this PSA and give the animal a name.

Storytime (Last Ten Minutes)

Ask the kids to return to the floor and invite them to come one by one to share their rewritten "public service announcements." Applaud them for their creativity and ability to see themselves from the small animal's point of view. Compliment them each time they make themselves into a scary monster with their use of language, and praise them for making creative changes to the illustrations.

Eyebrow ....

_____

_____

Arm ....•

_____

_____

Leg ....•

_____

_____

•.. Eye

_____

_____

•.. Stomach

_____

_____

•.. Hair

_____

_____

Ear ....•

_____

_____

•.. Neck

_____

_____

Foot ....•

_____

_____

•.. Knee

_____

_____

This public service announcement was brought to you by:

_____

VERBS THAT WOULD SCARE A SMALL ANIMAL

Crush	Yank
Stomp	Pull
Slap	Twist
Spray	Chase
Swat	Hunt
Pinch	Gobble
Trap	Swipe
Plot	Jerk
Drop	Sweep
Squeeze	Smash
Grab	Destroy

17

DIARY OF A T. REX

FEATURED BOOK

FEATURED BOOK

Diary of a Wombat
by Jackie French and Bruce Whatley

Length: About one hour

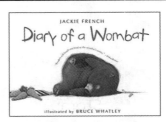

PR Blurb

After reading *Diary of a Wombat* by Jackie French and Bruce Whatley, kids will imagine the daily life of other animals—living, dead, or imaginary—and write diary entries from the animals' point of view. (**CCSS.ELA-LITERACY.W.2.3, CCSS.ELA-LITERACY.RL.2.6, CCSS.ELA-LITERACY.RL.2.7**)

In *Diary of a Wombat,* a wombat describes life with her "new neighbors," a human family that has moved into the area where she usually sleeps all day, in brief but funny entries. She describes how she manages to get carrots from the humans by scratching on their door, chewing a hole in the door, and banging loudly on the trash can. She tells the story of her fierce battle with the "flat, hairy creature" (the welcome mat) that was invading her territory. For her bravery, she receives a carrot. She decides that humans make "quite good pets."

Storytime (First Ten Minutes)

Invite the kids to take a seat on the floor and listen as you read *Diary of a Wombat.* Ask them questions while you read, such as: What was the "soft ground" the wombat kept digging in? How do you think the human neighbors feel about this wombat? What would you do if you found that an animal had chewed right through your door?

Group Writing (Next Twenty Minutes)

This writing activity can work very well as an extension of any curriculum you've done recently on animals. Using the whiteboard or flip chart pad, ask the kids what their favorite animals are—living, dead, or imaginary! If you have any dinosaur enthusiasts, you could talk about an animal like T. rex or a velociraptor. What would a normal day be like for her? What would be the first thing she does when she wakes up in the morning (or in the evening, if she is nocturnal)? What would she be doing by the afternoon, and what would be the last thing she does before going to sleep? It's okay if you don't know for sure what that animal would be doing; just imagine it.

Map out a normal, ordinary day for your animal. Model this for the kids by writing it out on the first page of one of the diary books that the kids will write in individually. Talk about the past tense, and explain that diary entries are usually written about things that have already happened to a person. Ask the kids if any of them keeps a diary.

Then remind the kids that they're not just going to be writing diaries for an animal, but they're going to make those diaries tell a story worth reading. It's going to be an *epistolary* story, meaning a story that is told using a bunch of documents, such as diary entries or letters.

All stories need to have conflict in order to be interesting. Something has to disrupt your animal's routine and be worth writing about. In *Diary of a Wombat,* the first few pages are boring because all the wombat does is eat and sleep. It isn't until the humans disrupt her environment, introducing new goals (getting carrots) and conflicts (someone filled in my hole), that things start to get interesting.

So whom should your animal encounter that will lead to a situation in which there is some conflict? Perhaps your T. rex will start getting competition from a feisty velociraptor who needs to be put back in his place. And then one day, he might notice a big fiery ball in the sky that seems to get bigger and bigger each day . . .

Individual Writing (Next Twenty Minutes)

Ask the kids to take a seat at the tables, and pass out the diaries. Invite the kids to write from the point of view of any animal or creature they like. They will be writing in

- » First person (in the animal's own voice using "I," "me," etc.)
- » Past tense (telling things that happened to the animal or things that the animal did)

Discuss these terms with the kids if they are unfamiliar. If you have English language learners, use the vocabulary sheet provided to help them find and use common past-tense verbs. This lesson will dovetail very nicely with any lessons they've had on daily routines or on irregular verb conjugation.

On "Monday," the kids need to establish the creature's normal, ordinary routine. On "Tuesday," something interesting should happen. The animal should meet another animal or have a problem. On "Wednesday," the problem should get worse. On "Thursday," the animal should deal with this problem or perhaps adjust to it.

Storytime (Last Ten Minutes)

Ask the kids to return to the floor. Invite them to come one by one to the storyteller's chair and read their animal diaries. Applaud them on introducing conflict in the animal's normal routine and showing how the animal felt about this change.

MONDAY (A Normal Day)

Morning:

_____

_____

Afternoon:

_____

_____

Evening:

_____

_____

TUESDAY (Something Happens)

Morning:

_____

_____

Afternoon:

_____

_____

Evening:

_____

_____

WEDNESDAY (It Gets Worse)

Morning:

_____

_____

Afternoon:

_____

_____

Evening:

_____

_____

THURSDAY (Problem Solved)

Morning:

_____

_____

Afternoon:

_____

_____

Evening:

_____

_____

PAST TENSE WORDS FOR DIARY ENTRIES

I woke up	I ran
I got up	I swam
I bathed	I flew
I ate	I heard
I drank	I saw
I looked	I smelled
I learned	I felt
I chose	I slept
I spoke	I dozed
I walked	I napped
I went	

NOTES

1. Deborah Wells Rowe, Joanne Deal Fitch, and Alyson Smith Bass, "Toy Stories as Opportunities for Imagination and Reflection in Writer's Workshop," *Language Arts* 80, no. 5 (2003): 369–70.
2. Bank Street Bookstore, "'If I Had a Raptor' and 'Olympians' with George O'Connor," YouTube video, 3:56, March 9, 2015, https://www.youtube.com/watch?v=7GgR3qACyZI.
3. Devin Karambelas, "Study: Students Prefer Real Classrooms Over Virtual," *USA Today,* June 11, 2013, www.usatoday.com/story/news/nation/2013/06/11/real-classrooms-better-than-virtual/2412401/.

The Plot Thickens

When I was a kid, I remember struggling with the concept of plot. Wasn't it enough, I wondered, for my story to have a "beginning, middle, and end"? I figured as long as I had "Once upon a time," "The end," and something in between, I had a story!

I didn't understand that my stories needed to have a problem. A story couldn't just be about putting characters in a pretty setting and telling all the fun they had during their day. It couldn't be all happy. It had to have a problem and resolve that problem in order to be considered truly a *story*.

For this reason I caution educators not to use the words *beginning, middle,* and *end* when explaining to kids the building blocks of plot. I'm sure that people use those words because they are simple and concrete. The words I suggest in their place are certainly more complex. But if you commit to giving children a more sophisticated concept of what makes a story and reinforce that concept again and again, I think you will be surprised how quickly your kids catch on.

In place of *beginning, middle,* and *end,* I suggest using the words *setup, problem,* and *resolution.* These words will convey to children the importance of conflict in storytelling and the fact that satisfying stories set up their conflict nicely beforehand and then resolve that conflict by the end.

Certainly words like *setup* and *resolution* may need to be defined for primary-grade students. I like to urge kids to see the word *solution* in *resolution* and reflect that in some way a problem is being solved and a satisfying conclusion is being reached. If you would like a visual tool for teaching these words, you can copy and print the pages in appendix B to post on your whiteboard. These pages contain questions that you can ask the kids in order to discuss how stories work.

BUILDING WITH CONFLICT AS A CORNERSTONE

The lessons in this chapter will encourage kids to develop plots that are about more than just a beginning, a middle, and an end. Kids will understand that conflict and tension are the elements that drive every good story. They will be challenged to show their characters solving problems. They will learn some of the conventions of various genres. They will learn about heroes and villains and the importance of having a compelling difficulty for their heroes to overcome or a powerful enemy for them to fight. They will learn about creating suspense by making sure that it isn't too easy for their protagonist to get what she wants. Finally, they will emerge from these lessons with a better understanding of the structure of stories, which will positively impact their ability to make predictions when reading and their ability to summarize the stories they have read.[1]

COMMON CORE STANDARDS

CCSS.ELA-LITERACY.W.2.3: Write narratives in which they recount a well-elaborated event or short sequence of events, include details to describe actions, thoughts, and feelings, use temporal words to signal event order, and provide a sense of closure.

CCSS.ELA-LITERACY.W.2.5: With guidance and support from adults and peers, focus on a topic and strengthen writing as needed by revising and editing.

CCSS.ELA-LITERACY.W.2.6: With guidance and support from adults, use a variety of digital tools to produce and publish writing, including in collaboration with peers.

CCSS.ELA-LITERACY.RL.2.3: Describe how characters in a story respond to major events and challenges.

CHICKENS CAN'T SING

FEATURED BOOK

Giraffes Can't Dance
by Giles Andreae, illustrated by Guy Parker-Rees

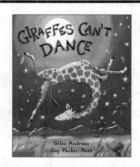

Length: About one hour and fifteen minutes

PR Blurb

After reading *Giraffes Can't Dance* by Giles Andreae and illustrated by Guy Parker-Rees, kids will create an unlikely hero and show how their hero rises above everyone's criticism to become a star. Kids will learn about the Hero's Journey and use it to create a compelling story. (**CCSS.ELA-LITERACY.W.2.3**)

In *Giraffes Can't Dance,* Giles Andreae and Guy Parker-Rees tell a delightful story in verse about an unlikely hero who goes from being the most scorned dancer in all the jungle to the best dancer and the toast of the town. Gerald the giraffe seems too clumsy and awkward to dance to the same music that the other animals enjoy, and everyone laughs him right out of the Jungle Dance. But after meeting a wise cricket that teaches Gerald that he might just need a "different song," Gerald listens to the music all around him and feels it in his bones. Gerald surprises everyone, including himself, when he begins dancing gracefully and beautifully. And he learns that "everyone can dance, when we find music that we love."

Storytime (First Ten Minutes)

While the kids are sitting on the floor, read *Giraffes Can't Dance*. After reading, ask the kids whether the animals' laughter and meanness make the kids want to give up on Gerald or root for him even more. Then ask them if they can think of any other unlikely heroes from movies or books who struggle with the criticism of other people and have to prove everyone wrong. Here are some examples you can suggest from movies that might be familiar to the kids:

- » Po—*Kung Fu Panda*
- » Ralph—*Wreck-It Ralph*
- » Judy Hops—*Zootopia*
- » Mulan—*Mulan*
- » Hercules—*Hercules*

Lesson on the Hero's Journey (Next Fifteen Minutes) ······················

The Hero's Journey, famously analyzed by mythologist Joseph Campbell in *The Hero with a Thousand Faces,* is a type of story that we see over and over again in literature, mythology, and film. It's a formula that works because it draws on basic truths about the human condition, because most human beings at some point in our lives have to

- » Learn from parents and teachers
- » Work hard
- » Overcome obstacles
- » Face our fears

All stories have to have some kind of problem or conflict, and the Hero's Journey gives us a formula for showing how a person resolves a really *big* problem. But because not all stories and films follow the exact number of steps laid out by Joseph Campbell, I like to give kids an abridged five-stage version that focuses just on those parts that kids will relate to the most.

Using the whiteboard or flip chart pad, write out the names of each of the following stages and discuss examples from *Giraffes Can't Dance* in which Gerald passes through these stages.

- » Stage One: Call to Adventure
  - The hero sees a need to leave his ordinary life and step outside his comfort zone.
  - *Example*: Gerald goes to the Jungle Dance.

- » Stage Two: Refusal of the Call
  - The hero doesn't think he can do it. He may be afraid, or he may be ridiculed by other people.
  - *Example*: Gerald leaves the Jungle Dance in shame and sadness.

- » Stage Three: Getting Help
  - Someone steps in and lends a hand, showing the hero that he is more capable than he thinks.
  - *Example*: Gerald meets the cricket, which tells him to find a different song.

- » Stage Four: Trials
  - Feeling better now, the hero goes to a new place and engages in an adventure of discovery and self-discovery. Sometimes the hero will struggle and find it difficult, but each new trial makes him stronger.
  - *Example*: Gerald hears a new song and starts dancing.

- » Stage Five: Success and Return
  - After the hero succeeds in accomplishing a major goal, he comes back home to find acceptance and admiration from his peers.

- *Example*: The animals find Gerald dancing and say he's the best dancer they've ever seen.

After exploring the ways in which Gerald the giraffe follows the Hero's Journey, ask the kids if they can think of examples from their own lives. When I do this workshop with primary-grade students, they often mention problems or fears such as riding their very first roller coaster or watching a scary movie. Sometimes they "refuse the call," getting to the front of the line for the roller coaster and then shrinking away in fear. (I have a vivid memory of doing this myself and feeling ashamed of my cowardice!) But they usually receive assistance, often from a parent, who gives them a bit of encouragement or wisdom to help them over their hurdles.

Brainstorming (Next Fifteen Minutes)

Ask the kids what they are good at. What talents do they have? Can they sing? Can they play soccer? Write down their talents on the whiteboard or flip chart.

Then ask the children to think of one animal that would have a particularly hard time doing each skill they listed. Make sure they can give at least one reason for naming each animal. Soon your list might look like this:

» Sing—Chickens can't sing—They only say "bok bok"
» Play soccer—Snakes can't play soccer—They don't have any limbs
» Draw—Dogs can't draw—They don't have opposable thumbs

Now for each of these problems, ask the kids to think of one mentor who might be able to help the animal accomplish that seemingly impossible goal. Your list will add new items like this:

» Sing—Chickens can't sing—They only say "bok bok"—But a nightingale might give a chicken voice lessons
» Play soccer—Snakes can't play soccer—They don't have any limbs—But Raúl could teach a snake how to "head" the ball
» Draw—Dogs can't draw—They don't have opposable thumbs—But an inventor could give a dog a device that will strap the pencil around her paw

Writing (Next Thirty Minutes)

Have the kids sit at the tables, and pass out the worksheets or books (templates can be found on our website). Invite the kids to adopt one of the suggested scenarios from the brainstorming exercise or come up with a new one of their own. At the top of the worksheet they should write who (or what) their hero is and what the hero's goal is. Then they will fill out the stages of the Hero's Journey showing that character move from ridicule and hopelessness to success and self-esteem. Remind them that giving the hero difficulties, like the problem of being made fun of by all his peers, helps the audience identify with the hero and root for him to succeed.

If you choose to use the books, I recommend giving the kids the worksheets as a pre-writing exercise—it will be very helpful in sketching out their plots.

Storytime (Last Ten Minutes)

Seat the kids back on the floor and invite them to come up one at a time to share their stories in the chair you used while reading *Giraffes Can't Dance.* Applaud the kids for coming up with ways to make the audience identify with their heroes. Compliment them on how well they apply the stages of the Hero's Journey.

Hero: _____ **Wants to:** _____

Step One: Call to Adventure
Where does the hero start? Does the hero have to go somewhere scary, do something hard, or learn something new?

_____

_____

Step Two: Refusal of the Call
Is it too difficult or too scary? Does the hero feel like giving up?

_____

_____

Step Three: Getting Help
Is there someone who helps the hero feel less afraid?

_____

_____

Step Four: Trials
Where does the hero go now? What must the hero do? How hard is it to do?

_____

_____

Step Five: Success and Return
Does the hero win? How? Is everyone else happy for the hero? How does the hero feel now?

_____

_____

19

PIRATE PUPPY

FEATURED BOOK

Battle Bunny
by Jon Scieszka and Mac Barnett,
illustrated by Matthew Myers

Length: About one hour

Supplies

» An overhead projector (recommended) or a laminated printout
(downloadable from our website)
» Dry-erase markers

PR Blurb

After reading *Battle Bunny* by Jon Scieszka and Mac Barnett and illustrated
by Matthew Myers, kids will draw over a boring artwork so that it tells a more
exciting story. (**CCSS.ELA-LITERACY.W.2.3, CCSS.ELA-LITERACY.W.2.5, CCSS.
ELA-LITERACY.W.2.6**)

In *Battle Bunny*, a boy named Alex receives a boring, babyish book called
Birthday Bunny from his Gram Gram. The book tells a clichéd story about a cute
little rabbit who can't find his friends on his birthday because they happen to
be throwing him a surprise party. Fortunately, Alex has a much better idea
of what makes for an interesting story than the fictional authors of *Birthday
Bunny* seem to have had. He rewrites the book as *Battle Bunny* and transforms
the narration, dialogue, and illustrations into his own story about a fearless
rabbit confronting all the horrors of doomsday. Although Alex's *Battle Bunny*
contains a lot of violence—one wonders if *Birthday Bunny* was a heavy-handed
effort at breaking Alex of his taste for violent stories—it's a relief to readers,
who likely won't be able to stomach the saccharine, unoriginal *Birthday Bunny*
any more than Alex could.

Storytime (First Ten Minutes)

Invite the kids to take a seat on the floor and listen while you read selections
from *Battle Bunny*. You won't likely be able to read the entire book cover to
cover in one group sitting. Select just a handful of pages that convey the story
of *Battle Bunny*. I find it easiest for the kids to see the pages reproduced on a

PowerPoint slideshow or reflected with an overhead projector. Taking one page at a time, first read the "original" text of *Birthday Bunny* and then show the *Battle Bunny* page on the screen, pointing out all the ways that Alex changed the story.

Ask the kids if they think *Birthday Bunny* or *Battle Bunny* is a better story. Which one has more of a plot? Which one has more interesting characters and problems? Which one has more suspense?

Brainstorming (Next Fifteen Minutes)

Show the kids the cute little puppy picture that they will soon be drawing over. It will help if you have the printout laminated and show it on an overhead projector. If using a laptop, you can download the printout and open the image of our puppy in a Paint program for the kids to doodle in. Ask them if they can think of any additions to the puppy's appearance that would make him more interesting. How about five or six eyes? Would "Mutant Mutt" be a better name for him then? What if he had a peg leg and a patch? Would "Pirate Puppy" be a good, suitable name for him?

Invite the kids to come up one at a time to the projector or laptop and, using the dry-erase markers, draw one change to the puppy's appearance. They have to explain their change to the group and tell everyone a story about how it came to be.

When you run out of space on the puppy, have the kids go to work on one of the other cutesy animals. Then work with them to list, on the whiteboard or flip chart pad, some ways that the puppy and the other animals can interact in the kids' new stories. Will they be friends? Will they be at war?

Writing (Next Twenty-Five Minutes)

Have the kids find a seat at the tables, and pass out the handouts or books (templates can be downloaded from our website). Challenge the children to create the funniest, wackiest, most exciting new story, as different as possible from the original pictures.

The boys in your group will be in heaven! I've seen many students, particularly the boys, who will come to my writing workshop after school and not want to do any "serious" writing. This workshop makes goofing around with pictures an *imperative.* It's still about creativity, higher thinking, and important practice with literacy.

Storytime (Last Ten Minutes)

Ask the kids to return to the floor and invite them to come one by one to the chair where you read *Battle Bunny* to share their stories with the group. Prepare to laugh! Point out how much *better* or *more interesting* their pictures are than what they were given. Congratulate them on taking a boring story and making it funny and worth reading!

TITLE: _____

BY: _____

_____

_____

_____

_____

_____

_____

_____

_____

_____

_____

_____

_____

MAYBE IT'LL WORK *THIS* TIME

FEATURED BOOK

Stuck
by Oliver Jeffers

Length: About one hour

PR Blurb

After reading *Stuck* by Oliver Jeffers, kids will write stories that either prove or disprove the saying "Insanity is doing the same thing and expecting different results." Kids will write about heroes who need more than one try to solve their problems, using suspense and surprise in their stories. (**CCSS.ELA-LITERACY.W.2.3, CCSS.ELA-LITERACY.W.2.5, CCSS.ELA-LITERACY.RL.2.3**)

In *Stuck* by Oliver Jeffers, young Floyd puts the saying "Insanity is doing the same thing over and over and expecting different results" to the ultimate test. Floyd's sanity will indeed be called into question by readers—although his apparent superhuman strength will be much less debatable!—as Floyd persists in following only one solution for getting his kite unstuck from a tree branch: he throws stuff at it. After losing both his shoes and his cat, he grabs a ladder and . . . throws it. Convinced beyond all doubt that throwing things into the tree is the way to get his kite back, he tries throwing bigger things. Pretty soon a car, a lighthouse, and even a curious whale ("in the wrong place at the wrong time") are all stuck up there! Every time we think Floyd has stumbled upon a real solution to his problem (for example, when the firefighters come along and ask if he needs assistance), we find Floyd tackling the problem in exactly the same way. So it shouldn't be any surprise—and yet it is, because of Jeffers's expert writing and illustrations—that when Floyd gets hold of a tool he can use to cut down the tree, he throws it at the tree instead. By sheer luck, his saw knocks down the kite, and Floyd returns to playing, forgetting all about the people and animals still stuck in the tree.

Storytime (First Ten Minutes)

Invite the kids to have a seat on the floor and listen as you read *Stuck* by Oliver Jeffers. I like to ask the kids what Floyd could do with the saw before revealing that he throws it into the tree. Talk about the saying "Insanity is doing the same thing over and over and expecting different results." Ask the kids why that is true and how they would rate Floyd's sanity.

Group Writing: Revising a Bad Story (Next Ten Minutes)

Tell the kids you're now going to tell them a very bad story. Write the story in advance on the whiteboard or flip chart pad.

> *Setsuko is a superhero. Setsuko has a friend named José. José was kidnapped and locked in the safe of the most powerful and wealthiest villain in the world. Setsuko knew exactly where José was. She went to the safe, opened it with the combination—which she had—and then Setsuko was able to get José out. The End.*

What's wrong with this story? The kids will probably be bursting with critiques, but here are a few suggestions in case they need help getting started:

> » Setsuko is a superhero but doesn't even need to use her superpowers to get José out.
> » The story doesn't say how Setsuko knew where José was.
> » It doesn't say how Setsuko got the combination to the safe.
> » Wouldn't the safe be guarded?
> » Where is the villain? Overseas on vacation? Why is the villain not at home to catch Setsuko and throw *her* in the safe?

Ask the kids to retell the story with more adventure and suspense. The hero's problem should never be too easy to solve, because where's the heroism in an easy challenge? Ask the kids if they can think of at least three difficulties to introduce so that the story about Setsuko and José will be a little more interesting. Write the difficulties they suggest on the whiteboard or flip chart.

Group Writing: A Lesson in Comedy (Next Ten Minutes)

Ask the kids to suggest a problem for a hero to solve. Maybe she has to get across a river or over a wall. On the whiteboard or flip chart, list as many problems as the kids are able to think of.

Pick one of the problems the kids listed and, with their suggestions, write down at least two things their hero could try that would *fail*. If the hero needs to get over a wall, maybe first she could try standing on her horse, but the horse moves and the hero falls. So she tries climbing a ladder, but the ladder breaks. So then she finds a helicopter. And then?

Ask the kids if they think the hero could get over the wall with the helicopter. Then ask them, if the hero were Floyd, what would *he* do? Would he get in the cockpit and fly the helicopter over the wall? Or would he lean it against the wall and climb on it?

Ask them which would be a funnier surprise ending for the story. If they say "climb on the helicopter," then they are thinking like a comedy writer, exploiting the tension between what audience members expect the character to do and what they would never expect any sane person to do.

Writing (Next Twenty Minutes)

Have the kids take a seat at the tables, and pass out the handouts or books (templates can be downloaded from our website). The kids will write about a hero faced with a problem that will take multiple attempts to solve. They can use either one of the techniques discussed in this lesson, building suspense through a variety of approaches to a problem with varying degrees of success or setting up the reader for a surprise by using the same awkward approach again and again.

Storytime (Last Ten Minutes)

Ask the kids to return to the floor and invite them one by one to read their stories to the group. Congratulate them on setting up a problem and coming up with multiple episodes in which the hero tries to solve that problem. Applaud their humor or their cunning in creating suspense and surprise.

TITLE: _____

BY: _____

Setup: What is the hero's problem?

_____

_____

First Try:

_____

_____

Second Try:

_____

_____

Final Try and Resolution:

_____

_____

EVERY HERO NEEDS A VILLAIN

21

FEATURED BOOK

Baron von Baddie and the Ice Ray Incident
by George McClements

Length: About one hour

Supplies

» Basic classroom or office supplies (see props and their descriptions in the Group Writing section of this lesson)
» Photocopier (to make copies of the collaborative stories so each child can take one home)

PR Blurb

After reading *Baron von Baddie and the Ice Ray Incident* by George McClements, kids will practice creating heroes and villains that are well-matched opponents. (**CCSS.ELA-LITERACY.W.2.3**)

In *Baron Von Baddie and the Ice Ray Incident,* an evil genius spends his every waking minute trying to build robots to destroy the world (or at least devour all its sugary treats), while superhero Captain Kapow is always on hand to thwart the villain's evil plans and throw him in jail. Then one day, Baron Von Baddie accidentally freezes Captain Kapow with a freeze ray and discovers he no longer has to spend so much of his time trying to get out of jail. Baron Von Baddie fills the empty weeks eating donuts and making new robots. But without a Captain Kapow to avoid, he finds he has lost his motivation for being evil in the first place. Without an opponent to his evil plans, his life has become meaningless. Thus it is that Baron Von Baddie stays up all night putting his evil genius to work, making a heat ray to free Captain Kapow! Captain Kapow immediately throws the villain in jail, and Baron Von Baddie feels *alive* again.

Storytime (First Ten Minutes)

Invite the kids to sit on the floor and listen to you read *Baron von Baddie and the Ice Ray Incident.* Ask the kids which character they relate to the most: Baron von Baddie or Captain Kapow. Ask them who is the real hero in this story.

Group Writing: Design a Hero and a Villain (Next Twenty Minutes)

Get ready to do some acting! Choose one student volunteer and ask if that child will be the hero. You will be the villain. Lay out some props and tell the kids that each prop represents a superpower. You can use whatever you have on hand. When I did this workshop at the library, I happened to have some superhero costumes left over from a Free Comic Book Day event. But in some ways it can be more imaginative if you use props like "magic" pencils and "laser" scissors that can cut through walls.

Here is a list of possible props and their uses:

» *Magic Pencil*: You can draw anything and make it real. You can draw a door and walk through it.
» *Laser Scissors*: These scissors can cut through any substance—brick, steel, you name it!
» *Portal Book*: Open this book, say the word, and you are transported safely to some other place.
» *Superpowerful Super Glue*: This glue can put an opponent in a very sticky situation.
» *Paper Airplane*: This airplane grants the bearer the ability to fly.
» *Molecule Eraser*: Anything the eraser touches starts to disappear.
» *See-Through Tape*: This tape opens a window into any wall so you can see what's behind it.
» *Stop Everything Watch*: Make time stop for you.
» *Fortune Teller 500 Magazine*: Open it and read what will happen five hundred minutes from now!

For the magazine, use construction paper to make a new cover for an old, discarded magazine. You have the option of using these props with predetermined traits or asking the kids to come up with the superpowers the props possess.

Now give your hero everything except the Molecule Eraser. The eraser will be your superpower, as an evil villain trying to erase the library!

Begin by saying, "Muahahaha . . . I am going to erase the library, molecule by molecule and atom by atom! I am so evil! *How* could you possibly stop me?"

This question should indicate to the student volunteer that she needs to use a superpower.

When the volunteer has acted out overpowering you with a superpower, tell her to take away the eraser to finish the story and end the play. At this point I often say, "Well, that was fun! Of course . . . It wasn't a very long story. Hmm. The hero came and foiled my evil plan, and that's fine and good because we wouldn't want a villain to really erase the library. But as the villain, I had no way to fight back. And that's not fair. It's also not very interesting. Wouldn't it be more interesting if I could fight back?"

Ask the kids to decide which powers to take from the hero and give to you, so that the villain will be a better match for the hero.

Now act out your erasing-the-library scenario again, only this time when the hero takes your eraser, you can fight back, perhaps with your Stop Everything Watch or your Superpowerful Super Glue. Then the hero will counter with something else. The kids can make suggestions to the hero about what to do next. Pretty soon you will be acting out a much more interesting story.

I like to allow twenty minutes for this group activity. Writing anything can be a struggle for emergent writers, but acting things out is something most children do happily. Researchers recommend letting young writers play with props and act out their stories for at least twenty minutes.[2] Playing this way will give struggling writers an accessible "entry point" to the story while giving more advanced writers an important reminder that stories are really about *play*.

Writing (Next Twenty Minutes)

Have the kids sit at the tables and select a partner to work with on a story about a hero and a villain. Pass out the worksheets or the books, which can be downloaded from our website. The kids' creative juices will be flowing after the group writing activity, and they will probably be enthusiastic about working together on a project, too. They could each be responsible for creating one character, the hero or the villain, or they could just work closely together on the whole thing. When they are finished, photocopy the stories so that each kid can take a copy home.

Storytime (Last Ten Minutes)

Ask the kids to return to the floor and invite each pair to come up in turn to read their stories to the group. You can ask them to explain the hero's and villain's superpowers or discuss their drawings. Applaud them on creating characters that are well matched for each other and not too easy to beat.

TITLE: _____

BY: _____ **and** _____

| Draw Your Hero | VS | Draw Your Villain |

_____   _____

_____   _____

_____

_____

MEANWHILE

FEATURED BOOK

Meanwhile . . .
by Jules Feiffer

Length: About one and a half hours

Supplies Needed for Prep

» Exacto knife
» Snack bags

Supplies Needed for Program

» Tape or glue sticks
» Paper (11 by 17 inches or 8 by 14 inches)
» Photocopier (to make copies of the collaborative stories so each child can take one home)

PR Blurb

After reading *Meanwhile . . .* by Jules Feiffer, kids will discuss different genres and write a genre fiction story on jigsaw puzzle pieces. When they put their puzzle pieces together with those of a partner, they will have a story that bounces back and forth between two different plot lines. They will learn about keeping the audience in suspense by placing the switches in the most exciting places. (**CCSS.ELA-LITERACY.RL.2.3, CCSS.ELA-LITERACY.W.2.3, CCSS.ELA-LITERACY.W.2.5**)

Note: This program will require some prepping. It will be helpful to have a volunteer or aide assist you with cutting out and bagging the puzzle pieces before the program, so that the kids will not have to divide their time between writing and cutting. You might find the exacto knife helpful in cutting the designs because it may be easier than scissors. If you suffer from carpal tunnel issues (as I do), the exacto knife will save both your time and your tendons!

You might also want to do a sample version yourself, just to make it easier for the kids to see how the pieces should fit together.

In *Meanwhile...* Feiffer's protagonist Raymond tries an imaginative solution to the age-old dilemma of having to put down your comic book because your mother needs you *Right Now*. By simply writing "Meanwhile . . ." on the wall (which I'm sure his mother is going to be *thrilled* to find), Raymond discovers that he can switch from the boring story line of his household chores to another, more exciting story line somewhere else! Suddenly he finds himself in a pirate adventure, living his dreams of climbing the rigging of a ship with a sword in his teeth. And anytime he likes, he can leave that adventure and trade it for another. There's just one problem: Raymond is constantly faced with mortal danger. When he is forced to walk the plank, he jumps into another story line, and suddenly he's dodging bullets in the Old West. He trades that one for an outer space story line and finds himself at war with a two-headed Martian king. Every story line he jumps into involves someone chasing him. Raymond proves himself to be quite the swashbuckling swordfighter, bandit, and interstellar warrior, but for all his heroism, he is always outnumbered and the odds are perpetually stacked against him. When Raymond decides he can take no more of this, he shouts, "The End!" In a wink Raymond is safe at home, where boring problems like an irate mom and a punctured, drippy trash bag seem so much more manageable than they used to be.

Storytime (First Fifteen Minutes)

Have the kids sit on the floor and listen as you read *Meanwhile* . . . . After reading, ask the kids which story line they would like to read more about. Do they want to know what happens to Raymond in space or if he gets eaten by the mountain lion? Ask the kids if they have ever noticed that books or TV shows always switch story lines or cut to commercials right when the story is getting exciting. Why is that?

You can also have a discussion with the children about whether they would rather read a story about taking out the trash or a story about walking the plank on a pirate ship. Is it a better story when the hero is safe or when the hero's life is in danger?

Genre Lesson (Next Fifteen Minutes)

Write the word *genre* on the whiteboard or flip chart pad, and give the kids a short lesson about what that term means. *Genre* can best be understood by kids as being a type of story that is distinguished by having certain settings, character types, and problems. The audience knows what to expect when they open a pirate book or watch a science fiction movie. They are not going to find the pirates joining hands and singing "Kumbaya." They are not going to find a fairy or a unicorn in outer space.

Usually, genre stories are able to expand the audience's expectations by having multiple subplots or story lines. This technique allows the writer more range to explore all the possibilities of the genre. But in order to make sure the audience doesn't get bored, the writer has to be careful to put the switch at the exciting places where the reader is waiting for a resolution to a problem.

Write a few genres on the whiteboard or flip chart. Ask the kids to help you make a detailed list of the characteristics of each one. They will most likely come up with examples of settings, characters, and objects found in each genre. They may need more prompting to determine what kinds of problems a character might encounter. Help the kids delve into what kinds of conflicts and dangers each genre presents; they will do better with the genre writing activity if they can identify at least two common problems for each.

Writing (Next Thirty Minutes)

Now that the kids have a chart of several different genres, they will go to the tables, choose a partner, and decide which genre they want to write about. They do not have to adopt the same genre as their partner. Whatever genre or genres they choose, they should each write a different character in a slightly different setting and doing different things. They could both write about the Old West, but one kid can write about a cowgirl on a ranch while the other writes about a bank robber in town.

Give each child a set of nine puzzle pieces cut out and placed in a snack bag. Each child will work independently for now. The children will write a Setup piece, indicating who their hero is, where the hero is, and what the hero is doing. On the Problem 1 piece, they need to introduce a threat or a problem. Resolution 1 will be a part where their hero solves that problem or escapes from that threat. But remind the kids that an adventure story is never about just *one* problem. Every time one problem is solved, another one arises. That's what keeps people reading. So they will need to write another threat on Problem 2 and the solution to it on Resolution 2.

They may want to know what they are going to do with all the pieces, but they need to focus on the writing for this segment.

Collaborating and Putting Puzzles Together (Next Twenty Minutes)

Once the kids are finished with their individual puzzle pieces, they will read their stories to their partner, and the two will work together to fit their two stories into one, alternating characters every time they come to a "Meanwhile" piece.

If two kids named Jayden and Natasha are putting their story puzzle pieces together, their final version should look like this:

- » Jayden's Setup
- » Jayden's Problem 1
- » Meanwhile
- » Natasha's Setup
- » Natasha's Problem 1
- » Meanwhile
- » Jayden's Resolution 1
- » Jayden's Problem 2

» Meanwhile
» Natasha's Resolution 1
» Natasha's Problem 2
» Meanwhile
» Jayden's Resolution 2
» Meanwhile
» Natasha's Resolution 2
» The End

Explain to the kids that, for the most part, the "Meanwhiles" should be placed in between problems and their resolutions. Just when one character faces a serious problem, the story switches to the other character.

Each child will have a set of nine pieces and will work together with a partner to assemble a sixteen-piece story puzzle out of the eighteen pieces they have in total. (There will be some "Meanwhile" and "The End" pieces left over—discard them.) When all sixteen puzzle pieces are laid out, an adult volunteer can tape the story onto an 11-by-17-inch or 8-by-14-inch piece of paper. Glue will take a while, but if you don't have volunteers handy, you can have the kids use glue sticks.

When the stories are fully assembled, photocopy them so that the kids in each pairing can take one copy home.

Storytime (Last Fifteen Minutes)

Have all the kids return to the floor, and invite pairs of kids to come up and read their stories. They can alternate reading the parts they wrote, or one person can read the whole thing. Applaud both kids on creating an exciting and long story with many different episodes and problems. Congratulate them on keeping you in suspense, waiting to see if their characters solved their problems.

Give yourself props for doing this, too! It requires more prep work than most of the projects in this book. Keep in mind, while you are doing all that cutting, bagging, and copying, that the kids are going to come away with really interesting, complex stories that they created together, as well as a deeper understanding of the intricate mechanics of storytelling. These stories will be ones they will keep and treasure!

NOTES

1. National Council of Teachers of English, "Professional Knowledge for the Teaching of Writing," www.ncte.org/positions/statements/teaching-writing.
2. Deborah Wells Rowe, Joanne Deal Fitch, and Alyson Smith Bass, "Toy Stories as Opportunities for Imagination and Reflection in Writer's Workshop," *Language Arts* 80, no. 5 (2003): 367.

Setup: Who is the hero? Where is the hero? What is the hero doing?

_____

_____

Problem 1: Oh no! Danger!

_____

_____

MEANWHILE . . .

Resolution 1: Phew! Your hero is still alive.

_____

_____

Problem 2: Oh no! Even MORE Danger! Even WORSE danger!

_____

_____

MEANWHILE . . .

Resolution 2: Phew! Your hero is safe!

_____

_____

MEANWHILE . . .

MEANWHILE . . .

Playing with Words

Every now and then, I'll be doing a writing program, trying to encourage kids to write about something important to them or a time they felt sad or their most cherished dreams or the like, and I'll get a kid whose only written answers to my questions are one- or two-word references to farts and butts. I never have a problem with kids writing stories about stuff like that, but I admit it can be discouraging when they aren't even attempting to write a story about it.

When I see this, I usually take a quick reality check: I look at the clock. What time is it? Almost always 4 or 5 o'clock in the evening. I remember that I'm doing an *after school* writing program, meaning that this child has *already* had to sit in class and think *all day long*. The other kids might still be full of enthusiasm and glad for the opportunity to write something creative and not academic . . . but not this kid. This kid is tired of thinking.

But writing doesn't have to be about thinking hard. It doesn't have to be work. Writing can be a game. Words can be tools for fun and play.

Language is a mind-blowing set of patterns, rules, mechanisms, and meanings, which can all seem daunting to a child. What's more, it's been around just long enough for most children and adults to get the impression that it is a fixed, unchanging thing over which they have no control. But that couldn't be further from the truth! Language is a living thing, and words are constantly being adapted and updated with new pronunciations, spellings, and meanings.

In these exercises, encourage kids to let loose, to take back the power of language and make it a toy! Let them explore what happens when they change one letter of an important word in their stories or when they mix and match parts of words to come up with an entirely new animal no one has ever seen before. Challenge them to make up new words and see where those words take them.

THE ROOTS OF READING

The exercises in this chapter will expose kids to new vocabulary as they learn about Greek and Latin roots. This knowledge will improve their ability to read and learn words they don't know. They will play with anti-rhyme techniques and thwart their audience's expectations to produce surprising humor. They will attempt a variety of different writing formats, such as riddles and poetry. They will learn about the parts of speech. They will read and write nonsense words, which are powerful tools in teaching kids how to decode real words. All these strategies will make their writing richer, while they are having fun!

COMMON CORE STANDARDS

CCSS.ELA-LITERACY.L.2.1.E: Use adjectives and adverbs, and choose between them depending on what is to be modified.

CCSS.ELA-LITERACY.L.2.1.F: Produce, expand, and rearrange complete simple and compound sentences (e.g., *The boy watched the movie; The little boy watched the movie; The action movie was watched by the little boy*).

CCSS.ELA-LITERACY.L.2.2.D: Generalize learned spelling patterns when writing words (e.g., cage → badge; boy → boil).

CCSS.ELA-LITERACY.L.2.4.A: Use sentence-level context as a clue to the meaning of a word or phrase.

CCSS.ELA-LITERACY.L.2.4.B: Determine the meaning of the new word formed when a known prefix is added to a known word (e.g., *happy/unhappy, tell/retell*).

CCSS.ELA-LITERACY.L.2.4.C: Use a known root word as a clue to the meaning of an unknown word with the same root (e.g., *addition, additional*).

CCSS.ELA-LITERACY.L.2.4.D: Use knowledge of the meaning of individual words to predict the meaning of compound words (e.g., *birdhouse, lighthouse, housefly; bookshelf, notebook, bookmark*).

CCSS.ELA-LITERACY.L.2.4.E: Use glossaries and beginning dictionaries, both print and digital, to determine or clarify the meaning of words and phrases.

CCSS.ELA-LITERACY.L.2.5.A: Identify real-life connections between words and their use (e.g., *describe foods that are spicy or juicy*).

CCSS.ELA-LITERACY.W.2.2: Write informative/explanatory texts in which they introduce a topic, use facts and definitions to develop points, and provide a concluding statement or section.

CCSS.ELA-LITERACY.W.2.3: Write narratives in which they recount a well-elaborated event or short sequence of events, include details to describe actions, thoughts, and feelings, use temporal words to signal event order, and provide a sense of closure.

CCSS.ELA-LITERACY.W.2.5: With guidance and support from adults and peers, focus on a topic and strengthen writing as needed by revising and editing.

CCSS.ELA-LITERACY.RL.2.4: Describe how words and phrases (e.g., regular beats, alliteration, rhymes, repeated lines) supply rhythm and meaning in a story, poem, or song.

CCSS.ELA-LITERACY.RL.2.5: Describe the overall structure of a story, including describing how the beginning introduces the story and the ending concludes the action.

CCSS.ELA-LITERACY.RL.2.6: Acknowledge differences in the points of view of characters, including by speaking in a different voice for each character when reading dialogue aloud.

CCSS.ELA-LITERACY.RL.2.7: Use information gained from the illustrations and words in a print or digital text to demonstrate understanding of its characters, setting, or plot.

CCSS.ELA-LITERACY.RF.2.3: Know and apply grade-level phonics and word analysis skills in decoding words.

CCSS.ELA-LITERACY.RF.2.3.D: Decode words with common prefixes and suffixes.

CCSS.ELA-LITERACY.RF.2.4.C: Use context to confirm or self-correct word recognition and understanding, rereading as necessary.

GO ON A WORD HUNT

Little Red Writing
by Joan Holub, illustrated by Melissa Sweet

Length: About one hour and five minutes

Supplies

» Paper bowls or plates (to make into word baskets for the kids to hold)
» Glue sticks

Note: This lesson will take some prep work, but it'll be that much more memorable for the kids! You may want volunteers to help you put the baskets together.

PR Blurb

After reading *Little Red Writing* by Joan Holub and illustrated by Melissa Sweet, kids will get word baskets and go on a hunt through the library for words to put into them, learning about different parts of speech. Then they will write a story with the words they chose. (**CCSS.ELA-LITERACY.W.2.3, CCSS.ELA-LITERACY.RF.2.3, CCSS.ELA-LITERACY.L.2.1.E**)

In *Little Red Writing*, a pencil named Little Red goes searching for a story to write for pencil school. She makes a plan and receives a basket of words to use in case she meets with any "trouble." She encounters all kinds of characters eager to help her polish her writing. She goes to a "Verb Action Fitness Program" to strengthen her prose and make it more active. She enters a "deep, dark, descriptive forest" full of interesting, chewy words like *gnarled* and *squirrelly*. She meets a well-meaning bottle of "Conjunction Glue" that accidentally causes her sentences to run on until she meets a new word: *Suddenly!* Unfortunately, "Suddenly" has brought danger with it, and she ends up following a suspicious tail leading right into Principal Granny's office. But someone growly and scary is posing as Principal Granny—the Wolf 3000 Pencil Sharpener! Fortunately, Little Red's word basket does contain a word that comes in handy for dealing with trouble—a stick of red "dynamite"! Little Red becomes the true heroine of her story and shares her writing with everyone in her class. This is a great book for inspiring writing and for modeling how transformative and fun a writing workshop can be.

Prep: Making Word Baskets ··

Making enough word baskets for everyone in your group takes some time, materials, and energy. This is a good project for a volunteer. To make the baskets, take two paper bowls (or plates if the plates aren't completely flat) and cut one in half. Flip the half bowl over the whole bowl and punch a few staples around the edges. You will get a rounded sort of basket with enough space to drop things inside or reach a hand in. (If you've ever made paper plate maracas for a storytime, this is very similar.) You can cut out a semicircle to make space for fingers to grip the top.

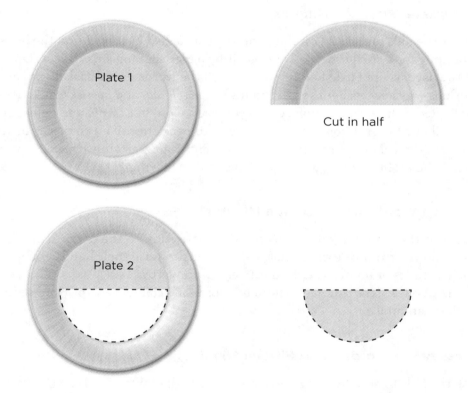

Staple a word basket sign on the front of each basket. The word basket sign will give kids a bit of instruction about the different parts of speech.

Prep: Hiding Words

Cut out the word strips. Depending on how many kids you are expecting, you may decide to make two or three copies. Copy them on a brightly colored sheet of paper to make them more findable. Before class starts, ask a parent or volunteer to hide the word strips around a part of the library or classroom that isn't being used during the storytime. Instruct the volunteer not to hide them too well—make sure they can be found easily, or you'll be finding random words tucked into your shelves for days afterward!

Storytime (First Ten Minutes)

While the kids are seated on the floor, read *Little Red Writing*. I find the book a bit long for a storytime, so I abridge it by paper clipping a few pages. Open to the page where Little Red is looking at all the words in her basket, and ask the kids why her teacher thought nouns like *maple leaf* and *lipstick* would help Little Red if there was trouble. Could you use a word like *cardinal* to defeat an evil villain? What if you got your cardinal to peck the villain to pieces or to tweet in the villain's ears until the villain went deaf? Certainly *dynamite* is an easier choice, but what if you didn't have a word like that?

Go on a Word Hunt (Next Ten Minutes)

Pass out the word baskets. Draw the kids' attention to the parts of speech listed on the front of each basket. Ask the kids to raise their hands and give you examples of nouns, verbs, adjectives, and adverbs.

Then release the children to hunt for words and collect as many word strips as they can find!

Classify the Words (Next Fifteen Minutes)

Ask the kids to stop hunting and have a seat at the tables. Pass out the Parts of Speech handout. Tell the children to sort (but not glue) their words in the boxes according to what parts of speech the words are. You can start by modeling a few examples and then move through the group helping the kids do this activity individually.

Writing (Next Twenty Minutes)

Pass out the story writing worksheet, and ask the kids to glue words to the top part and then use those words to write their stories. In *Little Red Writing*, the heroine is a pencil. Are there any other objects or animals that we don't usually read books about? Maybe it's time to write some!

Encourage the children to use at least a few of the words they found, but because you don't want to kill their creativity with strict expectations, be flexible. This activity can be the main one, or the top part of the worksheet can be a pre-writing exercise before the kids write in the books, which you can download from our website.

Sometimes I will get kids who just don't want to use the words they got. You can remind the children that sometimes having limitations or boundaries can be a good thing for creativity because it helps stretch their brains to make new connections they wouldn't otherwise have considered. This exercise helps them be more creative all the time! But let the kids know that this is free writing time and that they aren't being graded on it, so they can write anything they want. I never force the kids to write what I want them to write. I want writing to be a refuge of freedom that they can always come home to.

Storytime (Last Ten Minutes)

Have the kids sit on the floor. Invite them to come to the storyteller's chair one at a time and read the stories they wrote. Ask them to show everyone which words they incorporated, and be sure to applaud them on finding creative uses for their words!

A GUIDE TO YOUR WORD BASKET
Your word basket will be full of nouns, verbs, adjectives, and adverbs!

A noun is a person, animal, place, or thing.

A verb is an action word, something a noun does.

An adjective is a word that describes a noun.
Many words that end in "-ful" are adjectives.

An adverb is a word that describes
how a verb action is done.
Many words that end in "-ly" are adverbs.

Cut out these sixty word slips and make as many copies as you need for everyone in the class to get at least five.

ROPE	DRAGON	TEAR	RAPIDLY
KEY	CAR	GALLOP	BRAVELY
ROCK	OCEAN	BUILD	TIMIDLY
TREE	WITCH	EAT	SHIMMERING
SHOE	GHOST	THROW	FEARSOME
HORSE	STEAL	SHOUT	FRIGHTENING
DOOR	CHASE	DIVE	SPARKLING
PLANE	RUN	SWIM	BEAUTIFUL
TUNNEL	CLIMB	FLOWER	COLORFUL
RABBIT	TIE	CAVE	GIGANTIC
BEE	JUMP	SLOWLY	ENORMOUS
SCISSORS	BURST	DIZZYINGLY	MINUSCULE
STRING	HIDE	SUDDENLY	TINY
UNICORN	FLY	SURPRISINGLY	POWERFUL
BIRD	LEAP	ABRUPTLY	OVERJOYED

PARTS OF SPEECH

Nouns

Verbs

Adjectives

Adverbs

YOUR MAIN CHARACTER IS A:

> Glue a noun here

Your main character will | Glue a verb here |

in order to find the enchanted | Glue a noun here |,

the most | Glue an adjective here | in the whole wide

world!

Use these words, and at least one adverb, in your story!

_____

_____

_____

_____

INSECT LINGUISTICS

FEATURED BOOK

Du Iz Tak?
by Carson Ellis

Length: About one hour and fifteen minutes

Supplies

- » Wordless picture books (ten to twenty)
- » Sticky notes (sticky notes shaped like word bubbles are perfect for this lesson!)

PR Blurb

After reading *Du Iz Tak?* by Carson Ellis, kids will analyze the language Ellis invented for the book and use it to write dialogue for wordless picture books. They will add new words to the language, and, in creating new words, they will strengthen their ability to decode English. (**CCSS.ELA-LITERACY.W.2.3, CCSS. ELA-LITERACY.RL.2.3, CCSS.ELA-LITERACY.RL.2.6, CCSS.ELA-LITERACY. RF.2.3, CCSS.ELA-LITERACY.RF.2.4.C, CCSS.ELA-LITERACY.RL.2.7, CCSS. ELA-LITERACY.L.2.2.D, CCSS.ELA-LITERACY.L.2.4.A**)

Carson Ellis's *Du Iz Tak?* accomplishes an impressive feat—creating a made-up language for telling a story. Readers get a privileged glimpse of insect society, although the language the insects speak is not any known human language. A few insects happen upon a new green shoot and wonder what it is and what they could do with it. They seek out the advice of their friend Icky, who generously gives them the use of his *ribble* (ladder) to climb the green stalk. As you read, you start to be able to piece more and more words together as you notice certain words have a high frequency. With Icky's *ribble*, the insects are able to build an impressive *furt* (house or fort) using found materials. But danger comes in the form of Voobeck the spider—and a very *booby voobeck* it is!—who ensnares their *furt* in its web. The *furt* is saved by a bird who snatches up the spider. The insects rejoice and admire the growth of a beautiful budding *gladdenboot* (flower) at the top of the stalk. But as time passes, the plant becomes less able to sustain the *furt*, and the insects abandon it when the snows come. After a while, spring brings many green shoots just like the first. A new insect comes along and wonders, "Du Iz Tak?" Who knows—perhaps an entire insect city will be built from these new plants!

Storytime (First Ten Minutes) ···

Ask the kids to have a seat on the floor and then announce to them that they're in for an unusual story. Tell the kids that this book is not written in any human language on earth; it is written in the language of bugs. Challenge them to figure out what is going on even without any English words in the story.

While reading *Du Iz Tak?,* stop now and then to ask for the kids' help. Because you don't speak the language, how do you know how to pronounce everything? Perhaps your budding readers can help!

Revealing the Secret Code (Next Ten Minutes) ·······························

Now you're going to reveal the big secret you've been holding back: you actually *do* speak the insects' language . . . a little! I assume Ellis's book was written with an English syntax. Using that assumption I put together this translation key for the high-frequency words I was able to decrypt:

HOW TO READ INSECT

INSECT	ENGLISH	
du	what	
iz	is	
tak	that	
ma	I	
nazoot	don't know	
ru	we	
rup	our	
unk	a	
ribble	ladder	
badda	need	
su	yes	
furt	house, fort	
gladdenboot	flower	
ta ta	bye-bye	

Reveal this list (written out in advance and hidden on the whiteboard or flip chart pad). Tell the kids that it is a decryption key for understanding the insects' language. Using it, ask volunteers to help you reread selected pages of *Du Iz Tak?* and translate one page at a time into English. If there are any words the children still don't know, such as *booby*, suggest they make up the meaning using whatever information they can get from the context—the insects' facial expressions and body language, the presence of punctuation, the other words we are able to surmise. As the kids come up with meanings for words such as *booby* (maybe "ugly" or "bad" or "evil"), add them to your list.

Adding New Words to the Insect Language (Next Fifteen Minutes)

Now the kids have learned the Insect language! They can even read it! But it has fewer than twenty words. Show the children the following list (also written out in advance on the whiteboard or another sheet of your flip chart pad) of the twenty-five most common words in the English language:[1]

1. the	10. it	19. they
2. of	11. he	20. I
3. and	12. was	21. at
4. a	13. for	22. be
5. to	14. on	23. this
6. in	15. are	24. have
7. is	16. as	25. from
8. you	17. with	
9. that	18. his	

Can the kids translate all these words into Insect? Not yet. The only four of those twenty-five words with known Insect translations in Ellis's book are be or *is* (iz), *I* (ma), *that* (tak), and *a* (unk). That leaves twenty-one of the most commonly used English words. Your list is hardly complete!

Challenge the kids to help you to come up with new words to add to your growing lexicon of the Insect language. Tell them the fate of insect–human communication depends on it! Each child can volunteer one word to add to the vocabulary list. If there are more than twenty children, you could certainly add related words (like the different forms of the verb *to be*).

Your list will begin to look like this:

1. the—kug	5. to—eek	9. that—tak
2. of—bah	6. in—sig	10. it—lokumon-turokubot (because why not?)
3. and—dee	7. is—iz	
4. a—unk	8. you—wobe	

Writing Dialogue for Wordless Picture Books (Next Thirty Minutes)

Invite the kids to sit at the tables. Pass out the wordless picture books you were able to collect from the library. If you don't have enough for each kid to get one, have the kids choose a partner to share with. Give each kid at least ten sticky notes. Speech bubble or thought bubble sticky notes will be ideal for this activity. You can find them at office supply stores or online.

The kids will spend the first five minutes reading their wordless picture book and then use the sticky notes to add dialogue. (Remind the kids to be careful not to write directly on the book but only on the sticky notes!) For an added challenge, ask the kids to write this dialogue in Insect! They can use the words they came up with as a group, and they can go up to the board or flip chart and add more words as they think of ones they need. If a child is using Mark Pett's *The Girl and the Bicycle*, maybe she could change *girl* to *lob* and *bicycle* to *beekoo*. The new title would be *Kug Lob Dee Kug Beekoo*.

Here is a list of great wordless picture books you could choose from:

- » *The Girl and the Bicycle; The Boy and the Airplane* by Mark Pett
- » *The Lion and the Mouse; The Tortoise and the Hare* by Jerry Pinkney
- » *A Ball for Daisy; Daisy Gets Lost* by Chris Raschka
- » *Fossil; Chalk* by Bill Thomson
- » *Flotsam; Art & Max; Sector 7* by David Wiesner
- » *Good Dog, Carl; Carl Goes Shopping* by Alexandra Day
- » *Journey; Quest; Return* by Aaron Becker
- » *Inside Outside; Flashlight* by Lizi Boyd
- » *Bee & Me; Out of the Blue* by Alison Jay
- » *Flora and the Flamingo; Flora and the Peacocks* by Molly Idle
- » *Waterloo and Trafalgar* by Olivier Tallec
- » *Spring Hare* by Eugene Yelchin

Storytime (Last Ten Minutes)

Have the kids sit on the floor and take turns coming to the storyteller's chair to present their once-wordless picture books—now with Insect dialogue!

For added fun try this option: introduce a stuffed animal insect or an insect puppet to sit with the children and listen to their stories.

If you hear any new Insect words invented by the kids, invite the authors to add their words to your class lexicon!

HOW TO MAKE A BEAR BURRITO

FEATURED BOOK

Under a Pig Tree: A History of the Noble Fruit
by Margie Palatini, illustrated by Chuck Groenik

Length: About one hour

PR Blurb

After reading *Under a Pig Tree: A History of the Noble Fruit* by Margie Palatini and illustrated by Chuck Groenik, kids will write a silly recipe using a play on words. (**CCSS.ELA-LITERACY.W.2.1, CCSS.ELA-LITERACY.W.2.2, CCSS.ELA-LITERACY.W.2.5, CCSS.ELA-LITERACY.RL.2.6, CCSS.ELA-LITERACY.RF.2.3, CCSS.ELA-LITERACY.L.2.2.D, CCSS.ELA-LITERACY.L.2.5.A**)

Under a Pig Tree: A History of the Noble Fruit gives readers a hilarious glimpse into the behind-the-scenes process of getting a book published, as the author of a nonfiction book about figs goes insane with rage at the editor and illustrator of the book for changing *figs* to *pigs*. The author's frustrated comments, scrawled in red ink above illustrations of pigs being plucked from trees and pigs dressed as "Pig Newtons" with eighteenth-century wigs, reveal her growing outrage at the massive mistake being made with her book. There is also another story here—that of her editor's cavalier dismissals of her complaints, in comments written on sticky notes. Finally, M.P. can take no more, and she declares, "You people are INSANE! These recipes are for figs!" She spends the rest of the book drawing angry slogans all over the illustrated recipes for pigs. It is clear from the increasing morbidity of her drawings (roasting a dead pig and burning a copy of the book) that she may actually be losing her grip on her own sanity.

I've always had an affection for postmodernism and metafiction, and I'm grateful to be able to enjoy a book like this with my daughter. She and I just fell in *love* with *Under a Pig Tree* on first read, and we love to relive all our favorite absurd moments. My daughter's favorite is the recipe for Pigs Stuffed with Blue Cheese. "Give your pig a small pocket. Stuff it with a half-teaspoon of blue cheese." She can never get through that line without laughing.

Storytime (First Ten Minutes) ···

Read *Under a Pig Tree: A History of the Noble Fruit* to the kids as they are seated on the floor. You might want to abridge this book by paper clipping pages. Then ask the kids who they think is the more insane: the author (M.P.) or the editor or illustrator?

Brainstorming (Next Ten Minutes) ···

Write some foods on the whiteboard or flip chart pad in advance of the workshop.

- » Bean
- » Cake
- » Pie
- » Jam
- » Bar
- » Carrot

Ask the kids to suggest any animals that have names similar enough to these foods that it would be possible for M.P.'s editor to make a mistake with one letter. You can put the following pairings on the board or chart if the kids need a jumpstart:

- » Bean—Bear
- » Cake—Cat
- » Pie—Pig
- » Bar—Bat
- » Carrot—Parrot

Can the kids think of anything else those foods could be mixed up with? What about people's names? Perhaps your list will look like this now:

- » Bean—Bear—Sean
- » Cake—Cat—Cate
- » Carrot—Parrot—Carol
- » Pie—Pig—Pia
- » Bar—Bat—Bart

And how about these?

- » Flour—Fleur
- » Jelly—Kelly
- » Tart—Tara
- » Pear—Bear or Pilar
- » Oil—Owl
- » Jam—Ram, Jan, or Jim
- » Olives—Oliver
- » Milk—Milo, Malik

Ask the kids for their names and see if the group can come up with any foods that might be similar in spelling. For an exercise like this, I like to have Google handy, because it's not always easy to find foods for every name in your group! But it's okay if it requires changing or adding more than one letter.

- » Sally—Salad
- » Demond—Lemon
- » Gina—Ginger

Writing Silly Recipes (Next Twenty Minutes)

Invite the kids to come to the tables. After they have chosen one of the spelling pairings they came up with (or they can come up with a new one), they will write and illustrate a recipe for that food or for a food that uses that item as an ingredient. Pass out the handouts for them to write on. The handouts include some basic vocabulary they might need. It is not important for the kids to know exactly how to bake a cake or how to make a bean burrito, but if they want to do research, you can pull out some cookbooks from your library!

Instruct the children to write what the recipe is for at the top and write their own names on the line next to "From the Kitchen of."

Swapping Recipes (Next Twenty Minutes)

When the kids are done writing, ask them to swap papers with someone else and, using a red pen or pencil, write comments on their peers' recipes as though they are the angry author in *Under a Pig Tree*, demanding that the recipe writers stop being so ridiculous! You may want to model this interaction for them until they can pick up the practice on their own. Ask a student to volunteer a recipe, and copy a sentence on the whiteboard or flip chart pad. Then, in a different color, write comments such as, "What? This looks like a recipe for tossed salad, not tossed Sally! This is outrageous!"

If you have English language learners in your group, give them the vocabulary list and help them choose words that will convey their pretend frustration.

Storytime (Last Twenty Minutes)

Ask the kids to return to the floor and share the recipe they commented on if they thought it was really funny or absurd. They can interject with the comments they wrote down. Encourage them to be supportive of each other by asking them what they liked best about the writer's recipe.

Research has shown that beginning writers can benefit greatly from opportunities to interact with each other during writing, collaborating with each other and commenting on each other's work both orally and in writing.[a] Every such interaction is a modeling experience. When they see how their writing provokes a response such as laughter or surprise in readers, kids are more motivated to make improvements that will elicit a greater response.[b] This experience teaches them an important truth about writing—that "[a]ll writing is collaborative."[c]

Especially among English language learners, using an interactive model to write comments in the margins of students' writing has been shown to provide extra scaffolding and demonstrate writing and linguistic conventions. This approach promotes a level of engagement and conversation that is often lacking in other, more reductionist classes for English language learners.[d]

a. Efleda Preclaro Tolentino, "'Put an Explanation Point to Make It Louder': Uncovering Emergent Writing Revelations through Talk," *Language Arts* 91, no. 1 (2013): 16.

b. James F. Swaim, "Laughing Together in Carnival: A Tale of Two Writers," *Language Arts* 79, no. 4 (2002): 342.

c. Sharon A. Gibson, "Effective Framework for Primary-Grade Guided Writing Instruction," *Reading Rockets*, www.readingrockets.org/article/effective-framework-primary-grade-guided-writing-instruction. Originally published in *The Reading Teacher* 62, no. 4 (2008): 324–34.

d. Nadeen T. Ruiz, Eleanor Vargas, and Angelica Beltran, "Becoming a Reader and Writer in a Bilingual Special Education Classroom," *Language Arts* 79, no. 4 (2002): 298–99.

COOKING AND BAKING WORDS
(and Useful Ingredients!)

Stove	Tablespoon
Oven	Diced
Flour	Chopped
Sugar	Fried
Knife	Pastry
Measuring cup	Ladle
Teaspoon	Dough

INTERJECTIONS FOR ANGRY AUTHORS AND EDITORS

Outrageous!	Unheard of!
Ridiculous!	Ludicrous!
Absurd!	Preposterous!
Loony!	Bizarre!
Insane!	Unbelievable!
Crazy!	Incredible!

RECIPE FOR: _____

FROM THE KITCHEN OF: _____

_____

_____

_____

_____

_____

RIDDLE ME THIS

FEATURED BOOK

Guess Again!
by Mac Barnett, illustrated by Adam Rex

Length: About one hour

Supplies

» Scissors and crayons

PR Blurb

After reading *Guess Again!* by Mac Barnett and illustrated by Adam Rex, kids will write misleading riddles, using words and illustrations to help the reader make the wrong predictions. (**CCSS.ELA-LITERACY.W.2.2, CCSS.ELA-LITERACY.RF.2.3, CCSS.ELA-LITERACY.RL.2.4, CCSS.ELA-LITERACY.L.2.2.D**)

In *Guess Again!* author Mac Barnett and illustrator Adam Rex give us a well-executed, hilarious book of riddles no one could ever guess—unless, perhaps, you happen to be related to the speaker. Rex's misleading silhouettes are the perfect complement to Barnett's rhyming riddles, using various clichés and stereotypes to urge the reader in a certain direction. But the reader's predictions never turn out to be correct. After all, how could anyone possibly guess that the "floppy-eared" rabbit-shaped silhouette surrounded by carrots is actually the speaker's Grandpa Ned? Or that Grandpa Ned would look so similar to the speaker's *other* grandpa, Alan? The random absurdity of this book will keep kids guessing and giggling—that is, if they don't throw the book across the room!

Storytime (First Ten Minutes)

Invite the kids to sit on the floor and listen as you read *Guess Again!* While you read, ask the kids to make predictions and guess the riddles. How do their predictions change over the course of the book? On the last riddle, how likely are they to say, "Grandpa Ned"?

Lesson on Clichés (Next Ten Minutes) ·····················

One of the tools writers can use to urge readers to make predictions is the cliché, which gives readers a phrase or an image that is familiar because it has been used (overused, really) in many other stories. Write the word *cliché* on the whiteboard or flip chart pad and ask the children to name some clichés they saw in *Guess Again!* You can help them by suggesting one or two, such as the following:

> » Cats always getting stuck in trees
> » Rabbits loving carrots
> » Pirates having pet parrots
> » Bears invading picnics

Brainstorming (Next Fifteen Minutes) ·····················

Ask the kids to think of a person they know who might have an unusual habit or characteristic that reminds them of an animal. If the kids are too shy to volunteer, I like to volunteer my dad. I tell them my dad reminds me of a big, cuddly teddy bear! Then we list the ways that a dad could be similar to a bear. The list comes out something like this:

> » He could easily sleep through the winter.
> » He likes to spend time in his cave.
> » His back is very hairy.

Now in order to make the riddle in this example an extremely misleading verse, take it up a notch by including a word that rhymes with *bear*. Can you see any words in those lines that rhyme with *bear*? How about *hair*?

Here's my example now:

> » *He could easily sleep through the winter.*
> » *His back has a lot of hair.*
> » *He likes to spend time alone in his cave.*
> » *Who is he? You guessed it! He's my . . . dad!*

Ask the kids to make a list of other animal–people pairings. Remember, even though clichés should normally be avoided in writing, in these riddles the goal is to use clichés to trick readers into expecting what you want them to expect.

You'll soon get a list like this:

> » Teacher—hawk
> » Best friend—dog
> » Brother/sister—snake
> » Baby—monkey

Pre-writing (Next Twenty Minutes)

Ask the kids to sit at the tables, and give them the handouts. In the Pre-writing section at the top of the handout, kids will identify at least three similarities between their animal and their person and identify some rhyming words. Rove around the tables and help the children circle the one word that could be easily used to describe one of the three similarities at the top.

Writing (Next Fifteen Minutes)

Ask the kids to cut out the bottom part of the worksheet, then fold it on the dotted line like a greeting card.

Storytime (Next Ten Minutes)

Ask the kids to return to the floor and invite them one by one to share their riddles. Prepare to do some participating! Blurt out the name of the animal you are led to think their riddles are about, then act surprised when it turns out to be something or someone else entirely.

PRE-WRITING

MY ANIMAL IS: _____

MY PERSON IS: _____

Three things about my person that make him or her seem like the animal:

    1. _____

    2. _____

    3. _____

Three words that rhyme with my animal:

    1. _____

    2. _____

    3. _____

Circle one rhyme that you could use to show how that person is like that animal!

cut – cut

SILLY SPLIT-PANELS

FEATURED BOOK

A Cheese and Tomato Spider
by Nick Sharratt

Length: About one hour

Prep Needed

Copying, folding, and stapling the handouts into books, and cutting slits for pages to open in sections

PR Blurb

After reading *A Cheese and Tomato Spider* by Nick Sharratt, kids will make their own split-panel books while learning about parts of speech. (**CCSS.ELA-LITER ACY.W.2.5, CCSS.ELA-LITERACY.RF.2.3, CCSS.ELA-LITERACY.L.2.1.E**)

Nick Sharratt's specialty is making books that prompt pretend play and creativity, and *A Cheese and Tomato Spider* is one of my favorites for sharing with beginning readers. This novelty book may not be available at your public library, but I bought my own, and it was well worth it because it can be used as a tool for teaching lots of writing concepts. The split-panels yield over one hundred different, wacky exclamations that all work syntactically because their format is very basic and consistent: Interjection, Adjective, Noun. The illustrations fit together nicely, too, no matter how you combine them, and they are bright and large, perfect for sharing with a group. Children just starting to read can practice making different sentences while finding constant delight in the ridiculous phrases and pictures that they create.

Storytime (First Ten Minutes)

Ask the kids to have a seat on the floor and listen to you read *A Cheese and Tomato Spider*. I have a certain order I like to read it in. I like to do the wriggly ice cream cone, then the strawberry ice cream cone, and then the "strawberry flavoured" granny. I act weirded out by that last one and say, "Okay . . . , that's . . . nice, I guess." Then I turn the top flap to "A cheese & tomato granny," and I say, "Wait a minute—what exactly is this book trying to say? Is it suggesting I should eat my grandma? That's just evil! What do you think I am, a cannibal?"

Once the kids are laughing at that, I turn the top panel ("An exploding granny") and say, "Now that's just gone too far! Why does this book have it in for my poor granny?"

I also invite the kids to tell me which panel to turn, top or bottom. Sometimes they want me to read it again a different way, which I'm happy to oblige!

Mini-Lesson on Parts of Speech (Next Ten Minutes) ·················

Ask the kids what the words *spider*, *grandma*, *car*, and *volcano* all have in common. Give up? They're all nouns! Write the word *noun* on the whiteboard or flip chart as well as its definition:

> A **noun** is a person, animal, place, or thing.

Then you can teach the kids that an adjective describes a noun, and write that on the board or flip chart. Adjectives are the difference between a "big dog" and a "little dog" or a "blue car" and a "red car."

> An **adjective** describes a noun.

Write the word *interjection* on the board or flip chart and explain that the words "Wow" and "Eek" are interjections. They are exclamations that show you how the speaker is feeling.

> An **interjection** expresses a feeling.

Turn to some of the pages in Sharratt's book and ask the kids to identify which word is an interjection, which word is an adjective, and which word is a noun. Make a chart on the board or flip chart like this:

Interjection	Adjective	Noun
Ooh!	Sour	Lemon
Eek!!	Wriggly	Spider

Writing (Next Fifteen Minutes) ·················

Before class, prepare the books that the kids will write in by making copies of the template and stapling them together, then cutting along the dotted line. Do not cut farther than the line goes. This project is easy enough to give to a volunteer. You'll want to give each child four or five copies of the interior page template and one copy of the cover template.

Have the kids find seats at the tables, and make sure everyone has pencils and books. Encourage the kids to make the writing easier by choosing animals, objects, or people they enjoy drawing and by writing an interjection and an adjective on the top half of the page and the noun those words describe on the bottom half.

Illustrating (Next Fifteen Minutes)

Now pass out the crayons and markers and allow the kids to illustrate their books. Allow them to flip through *A Cheese and Tomato Spider* to get a feel for how Sharratt makes different illustrations fit together.

Storytime (Last Ten Minutes)

Ask the kids to exchange books with each other and read their partner's book! This activity gives them great reading practice, and the sentences will be simple enough for the earliest beginner. Move around the room and praise the children for their funny illustrations and phrases.

NOUNS . . . VERBS . . . WHY DO WE NEED TO KNOW THIS?

From time to time, I've had kids ask me why it's so important to know the difference between an adjective and a noun. I know a lot of adults who don't know the difference! Obviously, it's not of dire import to a person's survival, but I do wish more children started to learn what words are before they are expected to spell them accurately. Here's how I approach it. I ask the kids if they are writers and then tell them that all of them should have their hands raised because they are all writers in this workshop. Then I explain that writers need to know the parts of speech—the elements that make up sentences and expressions of thought—because writers need to be able to distinguish words from each other. What if an auto mechanic said, "Yeah, I know what the trouble is with your car. The problem is your what-cha-ma-call-it. It needs to be replaced, and your thingy-thing could use some more of that liquidy stuff"? Would you take your car back to that place, or would you take it somewhere more professional? In the same way, we have names for the different kinds of words we use, and we need to know those names in order to write well.

MY SILLY SPLIT-PANEL BOOK

By: _____

SCRAMBLED ANIMALS

FEATURED BOOK	ALTERNATE BOOK

Hello, My Name Is Octicorn
by Kevin Diller and Justin Lowe, with additional illustrations by Binny Talib

Scranimals
by Jack Prelutsky and Peter Sis

Length: About one hour and twenty minutes

PR Blurb

After reading *Hello, My Name Is Octicorn* by Kevin Diller, Justin Lowe, and Binny Talib, kids will make up strange new hybrid animals while learning a bit about Greek and Latin roots, prefixes, and suffixes. (**CCSS.ELA-LITERACY.W.2.2, CCSS.ELA-LITERACY.RF.2.3.D, CCSS.ELA-LITERACY.L.2.4.E, CCSS.ELA-LITERACY.L.2.4.B, CCSS.ELA-LITERACY.L.2.4.C, CCSS.ELA-LITERACY.L.2.4.D**)

Meet Octi the octicorn: the lovable though strange-looking offspring of a unicorn and an octopus. Sure, "kind of rare" might be an understatement, but the problems Octi has are much more common and universal than you might think. People are nosy about his background and how his parents met, and he struggles to fit in no matter where he is, whether with his unicorn relatives or his octopus relatives. He gets passed over when all the other kids are invited to birthday parties. But he is a mellow character with decent self-esteem, aware of the many things he does well, like playing ring toss and water sports. He's not so different from you and me. He even likes cupcakes—"because who doesn't like cupcakes?" The simple artwork and understated prose make this book a perfect choice to encourage beginning readers' creativity, and being able to draw Octi easily will boost young artists' confidence.

If you don't have *Hello, My Name Is Octicorn*, I recommend *Scranimals* by Jack Prelutsky and Peter Sis. These poems blend the name of an animal with the name of a plant or a food to come up with crazy new animals. The poems are excellent read-alouds, and the pictures are shocking—kids will especially laugh at the "Mangorilla"!

Storytime (First Ten Minutes)

Ask the kids to have a seat on the floor and and listen while you read *Hello, My Name Is Octicorn*. When Octi lists the things that octicorns like, and the reasons why the reader should consider being his friend, ask the kids, "Do you like the same things?" ("Octi likes s'mores. Do *you* like s'mores? Well, maybe *you* should be Octi's friend!")

When you finish reading, address Octi's question about why unicorns aren't called *unihorns*. That will lead you into a discussion about Greek and Latin roots.

Mini-Lesson on Greek and Latin (Next Ten Minutes)

So why *do* we call it a *unicorn*? Discuss the question with the kids. Tell the kids that, actually, the corn in *unicorn* has nothing to do with the corn we eat and everything to do with the horn on its head. Explain that most English words, especially the prefixes and suffixes, come from Latin or Greek. When you break down the word *unicorn* into its Latin roots, you get the Latin *uni* (one) and *cornu* (horn). *Cornu* is found in many words relating to horns, like *cornet* and *cornucopia*. Then share the etymology of *octopus* the same way. In this case, *octopus* is a Greek word—*octi* (eight) and *pous* (foot).

Write a table on the board or flip chart like this:

Animal name	Prefix	Suffix	Meaning of the whole word put together
Unicorn	uni (Latin for "one")	corn (Latin for "horn")	One horn
Octopus	octi (Greek for "eight")	pous (Greek for "foot")	Eight feet

Group Writing (Next Fifteen Minutes)

Talk about some other Greek and Latin words for animals, such as *rhinoceros* (Greek for "horned nose") and *hippopotamus* (Greek for "river horse"). Put a list of Greek and Latin numbers on the board. You can find a great list at http://phrontistery.info/numbers.html. Ask the kids to help you come up with a weird animal using Greek and Latin numbers. Ask them for a random number and a random body part and see what happens. What if you had an animal with six noses? What would it be called? In Greek, you might call it a *hexarhino*. What if it also had only one foot that it hopped around on? It's now a *hexarhinomonopus*! Give the kids a blank sheet of paper and invite them all to draw their interpretation of the animal.

Real Hybrid Animals (Next Five Minutes)

Although it is still unlikely that an octopus could have offspring with a unicorn, many other animals have been bred together to make interesting hybrids! Put the word *hybrids* on the board or flip chart and write this list under it:

> » Liger: half lion, half tiger
> » Geep: half goat, half sheep
> » Beefalo: half cow, half buffalo
> » Jaglion: half jaguar, half lion
> » Coywolf: half coyote, half wolf
> » Wholphin: half false killer whale, half dolphin

Kids might want to see photo examples, so have some printed out and ready to show them.

Make Your Own Hybrid (Next Fifteen Minutes)

Write the following on the whiteboard or flip chart before the workshop:

Dog	Cat
Squirrel	Lion
Otter	Horse
Fish	Whale
Unicorn	Porcupine
Octopus	Snail
Spider	Bird
Snake	Rabbit
Bear	Worm
Mosquito	Giraffe

Pass out the handouts and invite the kids to come up to the board or flip chart and select two animals, one from each column. They will write down the two animals in the "Mom" and "Dad" portions of the handout.

If you had an animal that was half dog and half cat, what would it be called and what would it look like? What about an animal that was half squirrel and half lion—a squion? Let the kids spend some time drawing their hybrid animals.

Writing (Next Fifteen Minutes)

Just as Octi argues for why you should be his friend in *Hello, My Name Is Octicorn*, ask the kids to make an argument for why this animal is a desirable friend. What can it do? Does it have any special skills? Does it enjoy the same leisure activities that kids do? Does it enjoy the same foods? Is it funny? Use the worksheets or books, which can be downloaded from our website.

Storytime (Last Ten Minutes)

Have the kids return to the floor and invite them one by one to come to the same chair where you read *Hello, My Name Is Octicorn* to tell the group about their new hybrid animal and make their pitch for why everyone should be the animal's friends. Focus on praising the compelling arguments each author makes for being the animal's friend and share why you would want to be its friend. Then invite group members to comment on what they like about the animal.

MOM

DAD

Created by: _____

HELLO
MY NAME IS

_____

_____

_____

_____

_____

_____

_____

_____

BRING A NEW ANIMAL TO DR. SEUSS'S ZOO

FEATURED BOOK	ALTERNATE BOOKS
If I Ran the Zoo by Dr. Seuss	*If I Ran the Circus* by Dr. Seuss *Scrambled Eggs Super!* by Dr. Seuss

 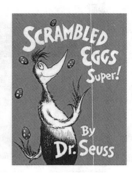

Length: About half an hour

Prep

See the instructions in the Word Wheel section of this lesson.

PR Blurb

After reading *If I Ran the Zoo* by Dr. Seuss, kids will spin a wheel to generate a new animal name and will create the look and characteristics of that animal. Then they will write a rhyming couplet about the animal. (**CCSS.ELA-LITERACY.W.2.2, CCSS.ELA-LITERACY.RF.2.3, CCSS.ELA-LITERACY.L.2.1.F, CCSS.ELA-LITERACY.L.2.2.D**)

Young Gerald McGrew is tired of seeing the same "old-fashioned" lions and giraffes at the zoo. He's certain that if he ran the zoo, things would be different. He'd take his job very seriously, traveling great distances to find the weirdest, most unique animals on the planet. Because who wants to see another boring old four-footed lion? You've seen one and you've seen them all! But not at McGrew's zoo—Gerald is certain he could find a lion with ten feet, five on each side. And if that wasn't already worth the price of admission, how about an Elephant-Cat? Or a Flustard? Or a Joat? Gerald's imagination knows no bounds, and he's out to build the zoo that will exceed anyone's wildest dreams.

I like to share this book and this creative writing activity when I go to schools for outreaches on Dr. Seuss's birthday. Read Across America (www.nea.org/grants/886.htm) celebrates Dr. Seuss's birthday by encouraging people to go to schools or host community events to read to kids every year on March 2.

You're probably already going to be reading Dr. Seuss to kids that day—why not bring a creative writing activity along, too?

Storytime (First Ten Minutes)

With the kids seated on the floor, read *If I Ran the Zoo* by Dr. Seuss. (You'll need to abridge it a bit.) Ask the kids which animal would be most worth the cost of their admission.

Word Wheel (Next Ten Minutes)

Before this workshop, print out the word wheel gears on card stock, cut them out, and laminate them. The word wheel gears were made using nonsense words taken from different Dr. Seuss books. Put the gears together so that the smaller circle with words sits in the center of the larger one with words and then the large circle with the window slit lies on the top and covers them both. Cut small slits in the center (I find folding the whole thing in half helps), and use a brad to fasten the three gears together right at the center of the wheel.

Ask the kids to have a seat at the tables, and pass out the handouts. Then pass the word wheel around, having each kid spin it until the child gets a combination of words. Each child should then write those words on the top of the handout where it says, "Your animal is a: _____-_____."

Writing (Next Twenty Minutes)

When everyone has two words, help the kids come up with rhymes for the second word of the two. You can do this as a group, writing rhymes on the whiteboard or flip chart, or by conferring with each kid individually. The words do *not* all have to be real words. Dr. Seuss often rhymed nonsense words with other nonsense words.

Then the kids will draw a picture of their animal. It can look however they would like. What would be their dream pet?

They need to answer questions about their animal, such as what habitat their animal comes from and what the zookeeper needs to feed it. This information will help the kids write a rhyming couplet about their animal at the bottom of the handout.

Show the kids some examples of rhyming couplets from the Dr. Seuss book you read. A rhyming couplet has two lines with the same number of beats and the same ending sound. Often kids aren't sure where to start, but I remind them that they already know a lot of words that rhyme with their animal.

Ask the following questions to help the kids write their couplets:

» Which of the rhyming words at the top might also describe your animal?
» Which of the rhyming words at the top might be something your animal could do?

» Do any of those rhyming words have anything to do with what your animal eats?

» Could any of those rhyming words have anything to do with where your animal lives?

Make sure the children understand that Dr. Seuss, when he was writing about the "Bustard / Who only eats custard with sauce made of mustard," chose those words very deliberately. It wouldn't have the same poetic effect if the Bustard only ate flies and spiders, would it? In fact, when Dr. Seuss was sitting down to write a book, he always started with a list of a few words and words that rhyme with them, which he called "the bone pile."[2] So, in effect, what the kids have already done at the top of the handout is create a "bone pile" of words that will help them write the couplet.

I often move around and suggest ways to word their couplets, making sure always to confer closely with the kids about what their animal is like and basing my suggestions strictly on something they came up with in another part of their handouts.

Storytime (Last Ten Minutes)

Ask the kids to return to the floor and invite them to come one by one to showcase the new animals they will bring to Dr. Seuss's zoo. Praise each child not only for finding a unique animal for Gerald but for giving him a great poem to advertise it to his customers!

NOTES

1. Edward Bernard Fry, Jacqueline E. Kress, and Dona Lee Fountoukidis, *The ESL Teacher's Book of Lists*, 3rd ed. (San Francisco: Jossey-Bass, 1993), 3.

2. Jessica Probus, "This Video Will Show You How Dr. Seuss Actually Created His Books," BuzzFeed, January 10, 2015, https://www.buzzfeed.com/jessicaprobus/this-video-will-show-you-how-dr-seuss-created-his-books?utm_term=.fbx3NegnG#.awkqRdyZ6.

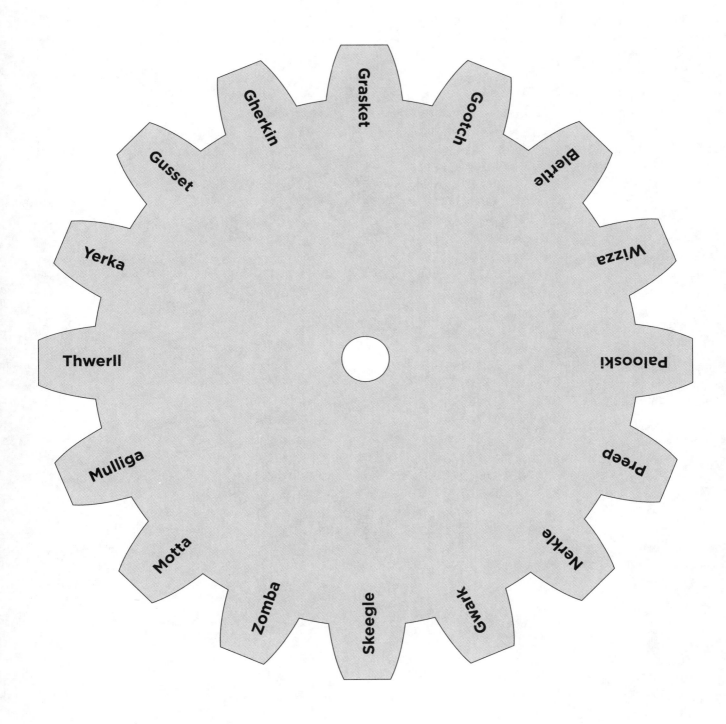

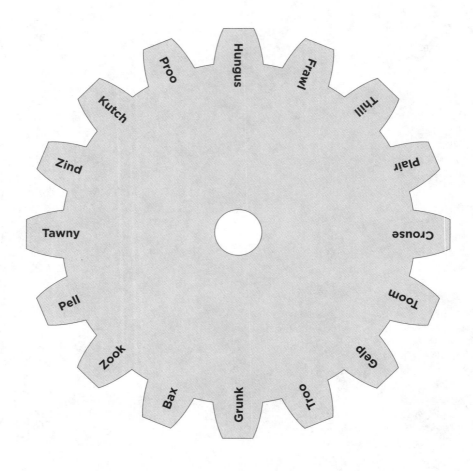

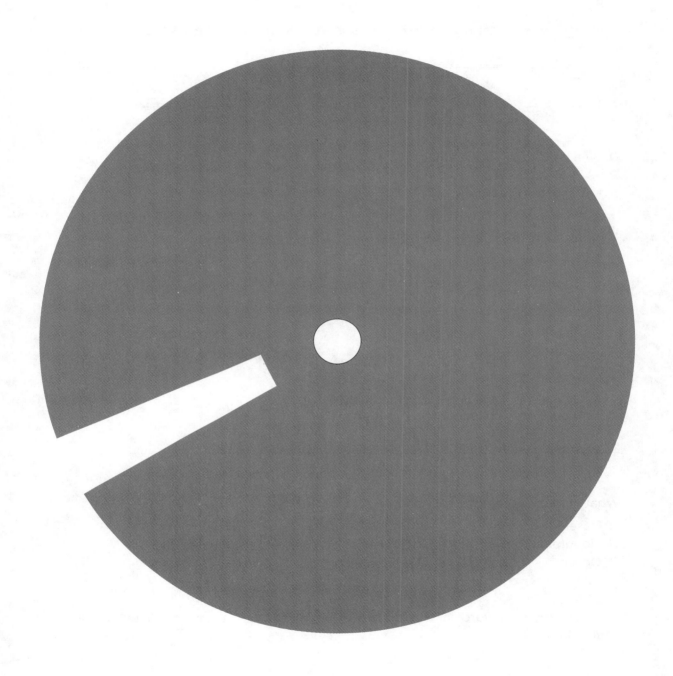

YOUR ANIMAL IS A: _____ — _____

Write four words that rhyme with the last part of your animal's name:

_____   _____

_____   _____

Draw a picture of your animal:

What would the zookeeper feed your animal?

_____

What kind of place does your animal come from?

❑ Desert   ❑ Prairie/Savanna   ❑ Jungle
❑ Mountains   ❑ Forest   ❑ Lake/River
❑ Ocean   ❑ Arctic/Polar

Using the rhyming words at the top, write a rhyming couplet (just two lines) about your animal:

_____

_____

CHAPTER SEVEN

Advertising and Other Forms

No matter what future lies ahead for our children, and what careers they will pursue, the ability to express the qualities of their products and services in an enticing way is an essential skill. In fact, a survey of midcareer professionals in 2003 showed that more than 90 percent of them felt that writing effectively was a skill "of great importance" in their daily work.[1] I would be shocked if the same survey today didn't produce even higher emphasis on the importance of writing, because in this era of the Internet and social media, every businessperson or entrepreneur must wear the hat of a marketer, knowing how to use words to convey quality and persuade consumers and stakeholders.

But alarmingly, American students are not entering the job market with those writing skills. In 2003, Hilary R. Persky, Mary C. Daane, and Ying Jin found that 70 percent of students in grades 4–12 were considered low-achieving writers.[2] If our children are going to be able to compete for the best jobs, they need to learn to have fun with writing and take pride in their ability to write.

MOTIVATE, SELL, AND SCRUTINIZE

In this chapter, we will explore some fun activities that will get kids writing in formats other than prose fiction and poetry. The National Council of Teachers of English in its position statement strongly recommends that children get experience writing "for real audiences" and "writing for a variety of purposes and audiences."[3] So in several of these lessons, kids will create commercial writing and then interact with each other's writing as audiences and potential "buyers." By expressing their preferences and opinions, their peer writers will learn a lot about what is most effective.

Through these exercises, kids will acquire more skills with persuasive and motivational writing. They will learn what kinds of diction will produce the most effective commercial writing for attracting consumers. They will also learn critical thinking skills as they get experience writing things that are persuasive but untrue. They will learn that you can't believe everything you read!

COMMON CORE STANDARDS

CCSS.ELA-LITERACY.L.2.1.E: Use adjectives and adverbs, and choose between them depending on what is to be modified.

CCSS.ELA-LITERACY.L.2.2.B: Use commas in greetings and closings of letters.

CCSS.ELA-LITERACY.L.2.3: Use knowledge of language and its conventions when writing, speaking, reading, or listening.

CCSS.ELA-LITERACY.L.2.3.A: Compare formal and informal uses of English.

CCSS.ELA-LITERACY.L.2.5: Demonstrate understanding of word relationships and nuances in word meanings.

CCSS.ELA-LITERACY.L.2.5.A: Identify real-life connections between words and their use (e.g., *describe foods that are spicy or juicy*).

CCSS.ELA-LITERACY.L.2.5.B: Distinguish shades of meaning among closely related verbs (e.g., *toss, throw, hurl*) and closely related adjectives (e.g., *thin, slender, skinny, scrawny*).

CCSS.ELA-LITERACY.L.2.6: Use words and phrases acquired through conversations, reading and being read to, and responding to texts, including using adjectives and adverbs to describe (e.g., *When other kids are happy that makes me happy*).

CCSS.ELA-LITERACY.W.2.1: Write opinion pieces in which they introduce the topic or book they are writing about, state an opinion, supply reasons that support the opinion, use linking words (e.g., *because, and, also*) to connect opinion and reasons, and provide a concluding statement or section.

CCSS.ELA-LITERACY.W.2.2: Write informative/explanatory texts in which they introduce a topic, use facts and definitions to develop points, and provide a concluding statement or section.

CCSS.ELA-LITERACY.W.2.3: Write narratives in which they recount a well-elaborated event or short sequence of events, include details to describe actions, thoughts, and feelings, use temporal words to signal event order, and provide a sense of closure.

CCSS.ELA-LITERACY.W.2.5: With guidance and support from adults and peers, focus on a topic and strengthen writing as needed by revising and editing.

CCSS.ELA-LITERACY.RL.2.2: Recount stories, including fables and folktales from diverse cultures, and determine their central message, lesson, or moral.

CCSS.ELA-LITERACY.RL.2.4: Describe how words and phrases (e.g., regular beats, alliteration, rhymes, repeated lines) supply rhythm and meaning in a story, poem, or song.

CCSS.ELA-LITERACY.RL.2.5: Describe the overall structure of a story, including describing how the beginning introduces the story and the ending concludes the action.

CCSS.ELA-LITERACY.RL.2.6: Acknowledge differences in the points of view of characters, including by speaking in a different voice for each character when reading dialogue aloud.

CCSS.ELA-LITERACY.RL.2.7: Use information gained from the illustrations and words in a print or digital text to demonstrate understanding of its characters, setting, or plot.

CCSS.ELA-LITERACY.RF.2.3: Know and apply grade-level phonics and word analysis skills in decoding words.

CCSS.ELA-LITERACY.RF.2.3.D: Decode words with common prefixes and suffixes.

CCSS.ELA-LITERACY.RF.2.4.C: Use context to confirm or self-correct word recognition and understanding, rereading as necessary.

GRAND OPENING FOR A LITERARY DINER

Dragon Pizzeria
by Mary Morgan

Length: About one hour and ten minutes

PR Blurb

After reading *Dragon Pizzeria* by Mary Morgan, kids will write a restaurant menu description of a celebrity-inspired sandwich that was created with a book character in mind. Then they will see if their workshop mates can guess the inspiration behind their dish. (**CCSS.ELA-LITERACY.W.2.1, CCSS.ELA-LITERACY.RL.2.2, CCSS.ELA-LITERACY.RL.2.7, CCSS.ELA-LITERACY.W.2.5, CCSS.ELA-LITERACY.L.2.1.E, CCSS.ELA-LITERACY.L.2.5.A**)

In Mary Morgan's *Dragon Pizzeria*, a pair of dragons named Bebop and Spike decide to open a pizza place that will make any pizza to order and deliver anywhere in Fairy Tale Land. They receive a series of call-in requests for unusual pizzas like "frog, snail and green lizard-tail pizzas," "teeny-weeny rose-petal pizzas," and "gingerbread pizzas with gumdrops on top." The reader is invited to guess whom these pizzas are for. Bebop creates the pizzas while singing songs styled after nursery rhymes, and Spike delivers the pizzas to addresses like "the castle in the Thorn Bush Forest." The rhymes are fun to do with a group, and the riddles are satisfying, drawing from a number of common European fairy tales.

Storytime (First Ten Minutes)

Ask the kids to sit on the floor while you read a few selections from *Dragon Pizzeria*. Choose a few of the customers that you think the kids will have the most fun guessing. Invite the kids to do the nursery rhyme or fingerplay with you, and ask them to guess before you turn the page and reveal the customer.

Brainstorming (Next Fifteen Minutes)

List on the whiteboard or flip chart which fairy-tale characters were featured in the book. Your list will include some of the following:

» The Giant from "Jack and the Beanstalk"
» The Witch from "The Frog Prince"
» The Bears from "Goldilocks and the Three Bears"
» Thumbelina
» Hansel and Gretel
» Sleeping Beauty

Ask the kids to name some other fairy-tale characters not on this list and ponder what those fairy-tale characters would want on their pizzas. You could start with these characters, not referenced in Mary Morgan's book:

» Snow White
» The Princess from "The Princess and the Pea"
» The Little Mermaid

How would you make a pizza that would signal to the audience that the pie was for one of these princesses? Here are some suggestions:

» Snow White: Apple toppings
» The Princess from "The Princess and the Pea": Soft, cooked peas—not raw, and not too hard!
» The Little Mermaid: Waterproof dough that won't get soggy

Group Writing (Next Fifteen Minutes)

Now ask the kids to name some other characters from books they have read. The characters don't have to be in a fairy tale, but they should be from a book. You could suggest characters like these:

» The Pigeon in *The Pigeon Finds a Hot Dog!*
» Fancy Nancy
» Clifford the Big Red Dog
» Pinkalicious

Ask the kids to vote on one character. Once the group has decided on one character, ask the children to put on their imaginary chef's hats and help you concoct a unique sandwich for your literary diner's menu, using that character as a "celebrity inspiration." Would the Pigeon want a sandwich with bits of hot dog, mustard, and chocolate chip cookies? Would Clifford need a fifteen-foot-long sub to fill his giant stomach?

Start by jotting down ideas suggested by the kids and then rewrite until the sandwich description looks like something that would be found on a restaurant menu. Ask the kids to refine the description with vocabulary that will make the sandwich sound appealing for any customer, not just the intended book character. Come up with adjectives that make the sandwich sound enticing and yummy!

Individual Writing (Next Twenty Minutes)

Invite the kids to have a seat at the tables, and pass out the handouts. Ask them to write any book or fairy-tale character's name in the top part and then fold the page over to cover up the name so that the kids sitting next to them won't see it. Then they will write a menu description for a sandwich inspired by that person.

Storytime (Last Ten Minutes)

Ask the kids to return to the floor, and invite them one by one to read the descriptions of the sandwiches they have invented—just the descriptions. Then see if anyone in the group can guess the inspiration behind the sandwich.

YOUR BOOK OR FAIRY-TALE CHARACTER

_____

Write the menu blurb for your sandwich:

_____

_____

_____

_____

_____

_____

_____

31

WRITE A CIRCUS POSTER FOR THE MOST HORRIBLE MONSTER ON EARTH

FEATURED BOOK

Little Rabbit and the Meanest Mother on Earth
by Kate Klise and M. Sarah Klise

Length: About one hour and fifteen minutes

Supplies

- » Tickets (the ready-made raffle kind you can find at a dollar store)
- » Tape or thumbtacks
- » Sticky notes numbered 1–30 (or the number of kids in your group)
- » Envelopes
- » Jar or box (for kids to drop their tickets in)

PR Blurb

After reading *Little Rabbit and the Meanest Mother on Earth* by Kate Klise and M. Sarah Klise, kids will create a circus poster advertising a terrifying monster, using hyperbole and superlative adjectives to describe it. (**CCSS.ELA-LITER-ACY.L.2.1.E, CCSS.ELA-LITERACY.L.2.3, CCSS.ELA-LITERACY.L.2.5, CCSS.ELA-LITERACY.L.2.6, CCSS.ELA-LITERACY.W.2.2, CCSS.ELA-LITERACY.RL.2.2**)

Little Rabbit and the Meanest Mother on Earth begins with a common conundrum: Little Rabbit's mother has told him that he cannot go to the circus until his room is clean. And like any other child, he thinks this state of things is terribly unfair. So he runs away and devises a plan to sell his own mother as a circus act: "the Meanest Mother on Earth." He sells a hundred tickets and succeeds in getting to be a part of the circus, but there's just one problem—how will he get his mother there? Now we see Little Rabbit's cunning as he blindfolds his mother and drags her to the circus where she will be showcased as a monster with "two heads" and "green teeth." But what does the audience see when Little Rabbit unveils his circus freak? A normal, ordinary rabbit mother who, like any other mother, just wants a clean house. The audience is furious, and I imagine Little Rabbit's mother is pretty shocked at the situation as well.

But she recovers very quickly and surprises everyone with a satisfying compromise, taking the whole audience back to her house to show them "something guaranteed to terrify." After their tour of "the Messiest Room on Earth," she invites them to take anything they like "as a souvenir." By the end of the book, Little Rabbit has fewer toys, but he's gained some wisdom. His mother has a clean house and a repentant son who will never try a prank like that again.

Storytime (First Ten Minutes)

Have the kids sit on the floor while you read *Little Rabbit and the Meanest Mother on Earth*. Ask them what they would have done if they were Little Rabbit, and what they would have done if they were Little Rabbit's mother. Why did she invite everyone to take whatever they wanted out of Little Rabbit's room? Was it mean that Little Rabbit played a trick on his mom? Does this story remind the kids of any other folktales about a person playing a trick on someone else?

Lesson on Superlatives (Next Fifteen Minutes)

Ask the kids to list examples from the book in which Little Rabbit exaggerates. Put the word *exaggerate* on the whiteboard or flip chart pad and explain its meaning. You can also add the word *hyperbole* and introduce it as being an exaggeration. Explain that hyperbole can be positive (such as saying you had "the best pizza ever") or it can be negative (such as "the meanest mother on Earth").

Then introduce some new words: *comparative* and *superlative*. Explain that there are different kinds of adjectives. Write a chart like the following on the whiteboard or flip chart pad:

Basic	Comparative	Superlative
Scary	Scarier	Scariest
Nice	Nicer	Nicest
Fast	Faster	Fastest
Big	Bigger	Biggest

Add more adjectives to the chart as the kids suggest them. If the word doesn't fit the "-er" and "-est" suffix model, then use it as a teaching moment to explain that some adjectives are irregular—for example:

» Bad—Worse—Worst
» Beautiful—More Beautiful—Most Beautiful
» Little—Less—Least

Now make a list of some of the exaggerated, hyperbolic adjectives used in the book:

- » Terrifying
- » Meanest
- » Ferocious
- » Shocking
- » Unbelievable

And phrases:

- » "Emporium of Odiferous Oddities"
- » "Mysterious Marvel of a Maternal Monstrosity"

Ask the kids to add new adjectives and phrases of their own to this list.

Drawing (Next Ten Minutes)

Invite the kids to sit at the tables and think about a circus monster they would pay big money to see. Give them the handout and ask them to draw in the center box the scariest monster, the most horrible monster, and give it attributes that would make anyone quake to look at it!

Writing (Next Fifteen Minutes)

Give the kids fifteen minutes to fill out the rest of their posters with words expressing how amazing their monster is. Make sure that they know they need to use really big, exciting words to sell this monster to their peers. They can use adjectives like "Shocking!" and "Astonishing!" and interjections like "Eek!" and "Wow!"

Showcase and Ticket Sales (Next Fifteen Minutes)

Using tape or thumbtacks, post the kids' circus posters around the room. Next to each one, place a numbered sticky note and an envelope. Give each kid two raffle tickets and show the kids the ballot jar. Tell the kids that these tickets are for the circus, but they can see only *two* acts. They will need to write the numbers of the two circus acts they would most like to see. I find that giving out two tickets encourages kids to do more than just vote for their own. I also remind them that their voting will be anonymous—the only thing the kids should write on the tickets is the number of each act they want to see.

Results of the Ticket Sales (Last Ten Minutes)

After everyone has written on their two tickets and dropped them into the ballot jar, drop the tickets each child earned into the envelopes you placed next to each child's poster.

The only thing I hate is for a kid not to receive any votes. If you are like me and want to make sure that all the kids get at least one vote, tuck a few extra tickets in the jar when no one's looking. Then if you come to the end and see an empty envelope, drop a ticket in as though someone voted for it. I know that's sneaky . . . but it's all in the service of making writing something that promotes self-esteem rather than reducing it. (Of course, if you're short on time, you could just have the kids drop their tickets into the envelopes of their choice, but that will remove the anonymity.)

Count the most popular acts and reveal the winners. Let them know that, because of their strong writing and imaginative pictures, their classmates clearly wanted to see their monsters. This kind of activity reinforces the concept of audience and gives the kids a "real-world" application for their creative writing.

MAKE A MENU FOR AN ICE CREAM TRUCK SHOP

FEATURED BOOK

How to Eat an Airplane
by Peter Pearson, illustrated by Mircea Catusanu

Length: About one and a half hours

Supplies

» Tickets (the kind you can buy in bulk for raffles)
» Thumbtacks
» Envelopes
» Sticky notes with numbers 1–30 (or the number of kids in your group)
» Ballot jar

PR Blurb

After reading *How to Eat an Airplane* by Peter Pearson and illustrated by Mircea Catusanu, kids will learn about the parts of a truck and come up with imaginative descriptions for how each part would taste. They will also learn about alliteration and expand their food vocabulary. (**CCSS.ELA-LITERACY.L.2.1.E, CCSS.ELA-LITERACY.L.2.5.A, CCSS.ELA-LITERACY.L.2.6, CCSS.ELA-LITERACY.W.2.1, CCSS.ELA-LITERACY.RL.2.4**)

As I've said elsewhere in this book, many great picture books start with a terrible idea, and *How to Eat an Airplane* by Peter Pearson and Mircea Catusanu proves that point well. Here, the "The Bad Idea Book Club" has created a manual for how to prepare, serve, and host an airplane dinner party in which all the courses consist of actual airplane parts! While kids are laughing at the idea of getting "a bolt or a screw stuck in your teeth," they also get lessons in table manners. The book is packed full of insights about being a gracious host, as well as fun facts about airplanes—like the fact that the fuel is stored in the wings or that "it takes forty-five minutes for the brakes to cool down after landing." The tongue-in-cheek humor and punny vocabulary ("Make sure to have plenty of knives, spoons and forklifts") make for guaranteed giggles. Bon appétit!

Storytime (First Ten Minutes)

Invite the kids to have a seat on the floor and listen to you read *How to Eat an Airplane*. You will probably hear a lot of "Ewww, gross!" during the reading. Kids, especially at this age, will want to express their shock at the images of children slurping up engine oil and chewing on landing gear.

You may want to look up some of the more esoteric airplane vocabulary in advance. I didn't know what exactly an "aileron" was, and I always like to be prepared for any questions I may have to answer.

Lesson on Vocabulary and Diction (Next Ten Minutes)

Using the whiteboard or flip chart pad, make a list of the food adjectives found in the book:

» Delicious	» Scrumptious	» Luscious
» Tasty	» Mouthwatering	» Rubbery
» Crunchy	» Succulent	

Ask the kids to add more adjectives to the list. Here are some other adjectives that describe food:

» Salty	» Tangy	» Aromatic
» Bitter	» Zesty	» Creamy
» Sweet	» Juicy	» Delectable
» Chewy	» Tender	» Flavorful
» Syrupy	» Rich	» Moist
» Spicy	» Fresh	» Savory
» Robust	» Hearty	» Sizzling
» Steamy	» Lip-smacking	» Sour

Ask the kids which of these words would make them want to try a chocolate cake. Would *sizzling* be a good word, or would *delectable* be better? Draw a little cake symbol next to the words that would work for chocolate cake.

Then ask the kids which of these words would describe a delicious cheeseburger. Would *creamy* work, or would *juicy* be a better choice? Draw a little cheeseburger next to the good choice words.

Explain that the kids have now developed a chocolate cake diction and a cheeseburger diction. Put the word *diction* on the board. Diction is, simply put, a writer's choice of words. Writers have millions upon millions of words to choose from, but they have to choose the words that will be the most effective and make the most sense. The same words that would work for selling a chocolate cake may or may not work for selling a cheeseburger. Choosing the *right* words is what helps kids develop a strong voice as a writer.

Lesson on Alliteration (Next Ten Minutes)

Now, you may well ask, how did Peter Pearson choose to call the seat cushions "succulent," the seat belts "scrumptious," and the tray tables "tasty"? Why *those* words? How does one know if a seat belt would be "scrumptious" or "bland"?

Pearson's choice of words demonstrates another kind of diction—putting together words that sound alike. Put the word *alliteration* on the board. A writer who makes a string of words sound nice together by choosing words that have similar beginning sounds is using alliteration. "Succulent," "scrumptious," and "seat" all start with the s sound, and putting those words together makes sense to us on a musical level, even if it's total nonsense on an intellectual level!

Another kind of device similar to alliteration can be found in Pearson's text: *consonance*. Consonance is the repetition of words that have the same consonant sound in their syllables. The phrase "mouthwatering windows" is not alliterative, but it has three w sounds in it—this is consonance.

Group Writing: Matching Vehicle Parts with Food Adjectives (Next Fifteen Minutes)

Invite the kids to sit at the tables, and pass out the worksheet containing a list of ice cream truck parts and their names. The kids are going to add food adjectives that will describe each of those parts. Ask them how they think the tires or the refrigeration unit would taste and feel. Be imaginative! Would the tires be chewy? Would the steering wheel be sweet? Would the freezer be zesty and cool? Do the activity with the whole group and write some of the word pairings on the board or flip chart.

- » Tires—chewy
- » Steering wheel—sweet
- » Cold plate freezer —zesty

Can the children think of any alliterative phrases? How about these:

- » Aromatic axles
- » Flavorful fuel tanks
- » Robust radiator

Individual Writing (Next Twenty Minutes)

Pass out the other worksheet and ask each kid to write the name of one vehicle part at the top. The kids can draw a picture of it on the plate in the middle. They can use any part they choose, and they can choose a different kind of vehicle than an ice cream truck. For example, if a kid is really interested in trains, she can write about part of a train engine instead. Have some books from your Transportation section at the library available for kids to flip through to get ideas and additional vocabulary.

Ask the kids to write a creative description for their vehicle part dish that would make someone actually consider eating it. They should think about how to describe the way that vehicle part would look, taste, smell, and feel—perhaps even how it would sound as someone is chewing it. They should make it sound *delicious*. If they get stuck on what words to use, suggest that they use alliteration, because alliteration always sounds yummy!

Be a Restaurant Critic (Next Fifteen Minutes)

As the kids finish their restaurant ads, hang up their ads and post an envelope and a number card near each one. When everyone's ads are posted, give the kids two tickets and let them move around the room and read all the ads. They can choose two ads they like best (anonymously), write the numbers of those ads on their tickets, then drop the tickets in the ballot jar. Remind the kids to vote for the most well-written restaurant ads that would make their mouth water!

Restaurant Ratings (Last Ten Minutes)

Ask the kids to return to the tables. Drop the tickets from the ballot jar into the envelopes for the ads they indicate. You can graph the scores for each ad, or you can just announce the winners. Remind the kids that all their ads were good, but there is something especially interesting and worth emulating about the winning ads, which the kids could learn from if they want to go into the lucrative business of advertising someday!

TIRE

DOOR

WINDSHIELD

SEAT

STEREO

REAR-VIEW MIRROR

BATTERY

STEERING WHEEL

MAKE A CAMPAIGN VIDEO FOR PRESIDENT SQUID

33

FEATURED BOOK

President Squid
by Aaron Reynolds

Length: About one and a half hours

Supplies

- » Laptop (connected to an overhead projector)
- » Video camera
- » Props (such as ties and bowties, or some small American flags)

PR Blurb

After reading *President Squid* by Aaron Reynolds, kids will review a few silly campaign videos and learn about the basics of making a campaign commercial. Then they will work in groups to write a campaign commercial for President Squid (or another animal of their choice) and film it! (**CCSS.ELA-LITERACY.W.2.1, CCSS.ELA-LITERACY.W.2.5, CCSS.ELA-LITERACY.RL.2.6**)

In Aaron Reynolds's *President Squid*, Squid gives the reader a detailed argument for why he should be elected president. For one thing, he wears a tie and lives in a big house. He is also famous (after all, anyone reading this book knows who he is!). He excels at bossing other fish around. And there's never been a squid president before, so he was destined to be the first! As Squid explains all his presidential attributes and tries to drum up local enthusiasm for his election, he looks around and realizes no one is even interested. They are all involved in their own problems, like the little sardine who can't hail Squid because he's stuck in a clam shell. Squid decides to do something about this and becomes an actual hero to his ocean community. There's just one problem now: helping people is a lot of work. Perhaps Squid has a different destiny . . . to be the lazy, all-powerful king of the universe!

Storytime (First Ten Minutes)

Invite the kids to sit on the floor and listen to you read *President Squid* by Aaron Reynolds. Ask the kids if it's really logical that someone should be president because he already possesses traits that sitting presidents have, such as wearing a tie or living in a big house. Explain that Squid is making a logical fallacy (affirming the consequent), believing that presidents wear ties and *therefore* anyone who wears a tie can be elected president.

View Some Campaign Commercials (Next Ten Minutes)

Tell the kids they are going to be working together on a campaign commercial to get someone like Squid elected president. They can write a commercial about Squid or another animal if they would prefer. They can write about their favorite cartoon character running for president or their favorite book character. Their candidate can be anyone.

To give the kids some inspiration, using your laptop and projector, show them some YouTube videos of silly campaign ads. I recommend the following:

> » *Alyssa Garmon's video ad for student body president:*
> https://www.youtube.com/watch?v=SxX8lDdZArY
> » *Payam and Sara's Student Council Campaign video:*
> https://www.youtube.com/watch?v=oyhuInkYbKo
> » *This Is a Generic Presidential Campaign Ad, by Dissolve:*
> https://www.youtube.com/watch?v=rouDIzhgVcY—
> a video about every presidential campaign ad ever made!

Ask the kids what parts of the videos were the best or the funniest. Was it funny when the high school students demonstrated their "strength" by doing push-ups? Or when the generic candidate showed lots of random people in different professions?

Ask also if the children can identify any common tactics that all the videos used to persuade viewers to vote for their candidate. (Review Aristotle's types of rhetoric discussed in lesson 4.) In general, campaign ads try to establish that

> » Their candidate is a morally good, trustworthy, and friendly person (ethos)
> » Some other candidate is the wrong person for the job (ethos)
> » Great things will happen if you vote for their candidate (logos/pathos)
> » Bad things will happen if you do not vote for their candidate (logos/pathos)

Campaign ads use fear tactics, mean gossip, cheap sentimentality, majestic sounding music, and dazzling smiles to get viewers to think positive thoughts about their candidate. Tell the kids to remember these things because they will need to incorporate different aspects of these videos in their commercial.

Small-Group Writing (Next Twenty Minutes)

Invite the kids to sit at the tables and form groups of three or four. Give the kids five minutes to decide who their candidate will be. (Remind them that it can be Squid, or another animal, a cartoon character, a book character—anything they like.) Give each group the worksheet with questions to help the kids brainstorm the important points of their candidate's character. Ask the kids to talk out their answers with each other. They should spend most of the next fifteen minutes talking, and one person can write down their answers to the imaginary voter's questions.

Rehearsing (Next Twenty Minutes)

Ask the kids to rehearse their commercials out loud and decide what they will say. They will have only two minutes for their film. They can read off the worksheet they filled out, or they can just use it as background material to give them ideas. Remind them of the things that they liked about the YouTube videos. Give them props to play with—maybe some American flags, ties, or a suit jacket. While they are acting things out, play a majestic movie soundtrack in the background to get them in the "zone."

Filming (Next Fifteen Minutes)

Film the kids' videos, group by group. You may need to take each group to another room or outside to be away from the noise of the rest of the kids. Set a timer for two minutes and try to encourage the kids to do no more than two or three takes.

Discussion (Next Five Minutes)

While you are importing the videos from your camera or recording device to your laptop, ask the kids to share with everyone who their candidates for president are and whether those candidates would beat Squid for president.

Campaign Ad Screening (Last Ten Minutes)

With your laptop connected to the projector, show the videos on the projector screen. Have everyone sit on the floor, dim the lights, and enjoy watching each other's movies!

When making your video, pretend that a voter is asking you these questions, and be ready with the answers!

WHO IS RUNNING FOR PRESIDENT?

_____

IS THIS PERSON GOOD-LOOKING?

_____

IS THIS PERSON NICE?

_____

HOW DO YOU KNOW THIS PERSON IS NICE?

_____

_____

DOES THIS PERSON HAVE MANY FRIENDS?

_____

WILL SOMETHING *GOOD* HAPPEN TO ME IF THIS PERSON BECOMES PRESIDENT?

_____

_____

WILL SOMETHING *BAD* HAPPEN TO ME IF THIS PERSON IS *NOT* PRESIDENT?

_____

_____

PROPAGANDA
The Truth about Flowers

34

FEATURED BOOK

Big Bad Bubble
by Adam Rubin, illustrated by Daniel Salmieri

Length: About one hour

PR Blurb

After reading *Big Bad Bubble* by Adam Rubin and illustrated by Daniel Salmieri, kids will discuss propaganda and fear-mongering and then get silly writing some propaganda of their own—a cautionary article warning monsters about the dangers of (harmless) creatures. Because in Adam Rubin's and Daniel Salmieri's world, monsters believe just about anything they read! (**CCSS.ELA-LITERACY.W.2.2, CCSS.ELA-LITERACY.W.2.5, CCSS.ELA-LITERACY.L.2.1.E**)

In *Big Bad Bubble*, Adam Rubin and Daniel Salmieri give us another wonderful read-aloud sure to elicit laughter and inspire admiration in young writers. The book begins with the intriguing premise that, when you pop a bubble, it actually goes somewhere else—to another world called "La La Land" where the residents, all monsters, see the bubble appear out of nowhere. These bubbles are quite mysterious and terrifying to the monsters, despite their own fearsome claws and fangs. After one monster named Mogo has a bad experience with bubble gum, he takes it upon himself to educate everyone else about the dangers of bubbles. Like much of the propaganda and fear-mongering writing we might encounter in our real world, Mogo's lectures and books are based on logical fallacies—even though he thinks he is just presenting "the facts." It takes a smart narrator, working together with a smart child reader, to show the foolish monsters through evidence and experience that they have nothing to be afraid of.

But some monsters never learn. Mogo, bent on selling fear to his fellow monsters, comes back with a new offering titled *The Truth about Butterflies*.

Storytime (First Ten Minutes)

Have the kids sit on the floor and listen to you read *Big Bad Bubble*. After reading, discuss how foolish the monsters are. Perhaps the monsters should learn not to believe everything they read! You can talk briefly with the kids about propaganda, which would be a great term to put on the whiteboard or flip chart pad—the word expands the kids' vocabulary while instilling critical thinking skills.[4] Propaganda is often political, but for the purposes of this lesson we could define it more broadly as *false* or *misleading information designed to push someone's agenda or opinion*. Mogo's book about butterflies is based not on evidence or experience but solely on his irrational fears. Because he attempts to scare his fellow monsters with false information through writing and pictures, his books about bubbles and butterflies can be considered propaganda.

Another conversation to have, which will be helpful later as the kids are writing, concerns the kind of tone the author uses. Is the narrator mean? Pushy? Nice? Friendly? How do the unseen narrator and the reader manage to convince the frightened monsters that bubbles aren't so bad?

Deconstructing (Next Ten Minutes)

Using a whiteboard or flip chart pad, help the kids deconstruct Mogo's lesson on bubbles to see if there are any truths behind his fears. Obviously, it would be weird living in a place where bubbles just appear out of thin air. But is there any other truth to the exaggerated claims that Mogo makes about the danger of bubbles? Take each claim one by one and write it on the whiteboard or flip chart pad.

Ask the kids if these facts are enough for Mogo to convince them that bubbles are evil. What facts is Mogo's argument missing?

Your list may look something like this by the end:

Bubbles are sneaky:
True? They are very quiet.
False? Bubbles don't have brains so they can't have any bad intentions.

Bubbles travel in packs:
True? When you blow bubbles, many come out all at once.
False? They don't travel together by choice. They just float with the wind.

Summer is the worst time for bubbles, a time when they go on a feeding frenzy:
True? Kids might be more likely to be outside blowing bubbles when it's sunny than when it's rainy.
False? Bubbles don't eat, so they can't go on a feeding frenzy. Also, how can we know for sure that more bubbles are blown during the summer? Has anyone studied the number of bubbles blown at other times of the year? Probably not. Could you design a science experiment to determine whether more bubbles are blown during the summer?

Ask the kids whether Mogo's drawings of bubbles are realistic or fantastical. Would you find drawings like these in a real science book about bubbles?

Brainstorming (Next Fifteen Minutes)

Ask the kids to suggest at least five different beings that are completely harmless to humans. When you have a handful of creatures written on the whiteboard or flip chart pad, add a few true characteristics of each one.

Using those characteristics as a starting point, work with the kids to list false claims that would make a monster scared of those harmless creatures. For example:

FLOWERS

True:
- They are colorful.
- They smell fragrant.

False:
- Their bright colors will destroy your eyes. Once you are blind, they will capture and eat you!
- If you breathe their poisonous smell, your lungs will collapse and you'll die!

Writing (Next Twenty Minutes)

As the kids move to the tables, pass out the worksheet or folded and stapled books (templates are provided on our website). The worksheet asks the kids to begin their propaganda article by finishing this sentence: "You might think that _____ are _____ , but did you know that _____?" Encourage the kids to make their first sentence sound as ominous and scary as possible so as to "hook" the reader. They should ponder their sentence's impact on their audience and do their best to make the audience read on in breathless terror!

Storytime (Last Ten Minutes)

Have the kids return to the floor and invite them one by one to read their articles or books. Applaud them on making chilling propaganda that would convince a foolish monster to wet his pants with fear. And then applaud them on being smart enough to know it's all just propaganda!

DANGER

Finish this sentence:

You might think that _____

are _____**, but did you know that**

_____**?**

DANGER

CAUTION

CAUTION

DANGER

_____

_____

_____

_____

_____

_____

CAUTION

WHAT WILL *YOU* DO WITH YOUR IDEA?

FEATURED BOOK

What Do You Do with an Idea?
by Kobi Yamada, illustrated by Mae Besom

Length: About one hour

Supplies

» Disposable tablecloth
» Watercolor painting sets
» White crayons
» Cups of water

(If you want to make larger posters for the kids to color, simply enlarge the worksheet and photocopy it on a large sheet of paper.)

PR Blurb

After reading *What Do You Do with an Idea?* by Kobi Yamada and illustrated by Mae Besom, kids will think about a dream they have and what steps they need to take to make that dream a reality. Then they will make an inspirational poster detailing those steps in such a way that their idea will emerge through the colors like "magic"! (**CCSS.ELA-LITERACY.L.2.6, CCSS.ELA-LITERACY.RL.2.7**)

There's a reason why people sometimes call a project or idea their "child" or their "baby." Like a child, an idea requires nurturing and love in order to grow. Yamada and Besom's book illustrates that concept beautifully in the funny little egg that follows the speaker around. The speaker hides the egg at first, fearful of what other people will think, but he cannot shake the hold his idea has on him. After feeding it and taking care of it, he falls in love with his idea. It grows bigger and more beautiful, impacting everything around it, filling the black-and-white-penciled world with color until the whole page is vivid and bright. This sets the stage perfectly for the main character's touching last line about how a good idea can change the world.

Many of the writers, artists, and teachers that I know have *What Do You Do with an Idea?* by Kobi Yamada and illustrated by Mae Besom. It's become a popular gift book to give to anyone working in a creative field. Although I think adults who have lived longer and struggled more may understand this book at a deeper level than most kids can, I love to share this book with kids who are just starting out so that they are exposed to its truths early on. From this book, kids can learn that the world isn't always going to love their ideas and that it's up to them to love their ideas themselves.

Storytime (First Ten Minutes)

Ask the kids to have a seat on the floor and listen as you read *What Do You Do with an Idea?* After reading, ask how the illustrator showed this idea changing the world. Discuss what the speaker meant when he said he gave his idea "food." What does it mean to take care of an idea? What would you do if someone laughed at your idea? Would you give up on it?

Visualizing Our Dreams (Next Fifteen Minutes)

Invite the kids to sit at the tables, and pass out some blank sheets of lined paper. Ask the children to close their eyes and think about what they would like to be when they grow up. They should not worry about being sensible or practical—they should think BIG. What would be their *dream* life?

Ask the kids to imagine where they are in that dream. What do they love doing? What kind of house do they have? What are they famous for?

Now the kids can open their eyes and spend ten minutes writing down as much as they can remember about that dream for themselves. Explain that the more detailed they can be about their dreams, the easier it will be to achieve them someday. The kids may not know this but Olympic athletes have been known to use visualization and dreams to improve their performance![5] If visualization works for someone whose dream is to be the fastest runner in the world, it's worth a try, no matter what your dream might be!

Idea Posters (Last Thirty Minutes)

Pass out the worksheets with the large egg picture (you can enlarge them if you would like), and give each kid a white crayon. Ask the kids to write their dream in just one word, in big, bold letters using their white crayon. No one else will be able to see what their dream is—for now, it will be a secret known only to them! Just as in *What Do You Do with an Idea?*, sometimes you need to protect your idea and keep it hidden or keep it to yourself, and that's okay. At some point you will be ready to share it with the world.

Now ask the kids to write (in pencil all over the egg) some actions they can take right now to help make that dream a reality. If a kid's dream is to be an astronaut, encourage him to think about what makes a person an astronaut. How does an astronaut *become* an astronaut? What does an astronaut do when she is not in outer space? Was there anything she did as a child that might have led to her becoming an astronaut? Did she watch TV all day, every day, or did she spend time reading books about science and studying for tests? Sometimes if you turn a child's attention to what a successful person probably does *not* do, the child will come up with more ideas for things *to* do.

Then a kid who wants to be an astronaut can write things such as these:

» Read more science books.
» Learn about rockets.
» Visit a science museum or a planetarium.
» Watch a movie about astronauts.
» Get better at math.
» Do well in all school subjects.
» Eat healthy food.
» Exercise to be strong in zero gravity.
» Practice building things.
» Learn to recognize the stars and planets.
» Save money to get a telescope.

This is a great opportunity to pull out your career books and biographies to help the kids identify the actual habits and practices of successful people.

Once the kids have covered their eggs with various actions they can take to make their dreams happen, ask the kids to think about which of these actions are about learning from other people. Which of these actions, if done well, will help the idea grow and lead to more knowledge and ideas? Personally, from the preceding list, I would choose "Read more science books," "Watch a movie about astronauts," and "Visit a science museum or a planetarium." Those things will feed my dream, inspire me to think more, and make my astronaut dream more detailed and defined.

Pass out the watercolors. Make sure the kids also have little cups of water for cleaning brushes. Tell the kids to start with green—for every action that will help their ideas grow and that will inspire them, they will brush over the words with green watercolor. This activity is like feeding their ideas healthy fruits and vegetables!

In addition to healthy food, their ideas will need exercise. Tell the kids to choose any color they like to paint over the words that involve exercising their idea. In the astronaut example, I would paint over the words "Practice building things," "Exercise to be strong in zero gravity," and "Get better at math."

All the things the kids listed should be painted over at this point. And once the egg is full of color, something new should emerge through all that paint—the white wax crayon word that the kids wrote at the start. Doing all those actions, and knowing how those actions either feed or exercise an idea, makes the idea stand out bright and clear, ready to be shared with the world!

Once their posters are dry, the kids can take them home, or you can post them around the room to give the kids inspiration the next time they come to write.

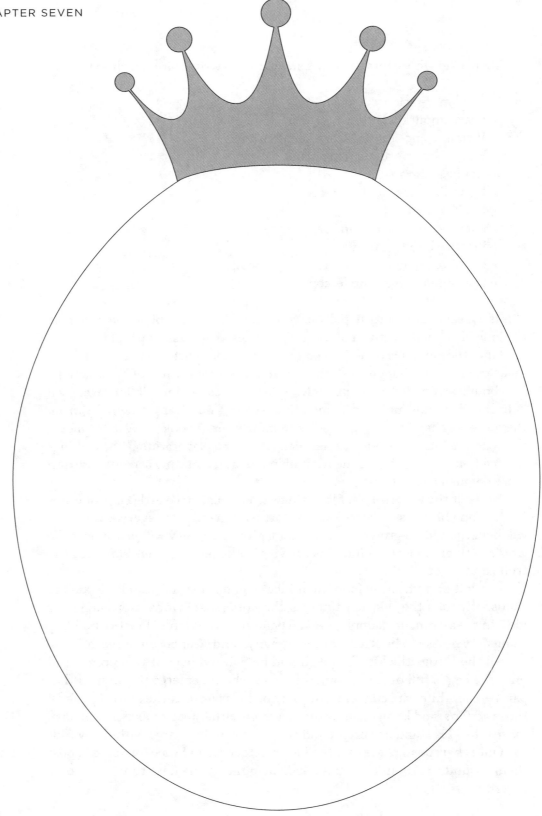

In white crayon, write your idea in huge letters on the egg. In pencil, write all over the egg the things you need to do to help your idea become real. If something feeds your idea healthy food like new knowledge or excitement, paint over the words with green paint. If something means working hard and giving your idea exercise, paint over the words with any other color.

MAKE YOUR OWN JAR OF HAPPINESS

FEATURED BOOK

The Jar of Happiness
by Ailsa Burrows

Length: About one hour

Supplies

- » Clean jars
- » Glue
- » Scissors
- » Decorating supplies (stickers, glitter glue, etc.)

PR Blurb

After reading *The Jar of Happiness* by Ailsa Burrows, kids will each fill a jar with the names of things that make them happy and then consider the way those things smell, feel, and look in order to create enticing labels for their jars. (**CCSS.ELA-LITERACY.L.2.1.E, CCSS.ELA-LITERACY.L.2.5.A, CCSS.ELA-LITERACY.L.2.6, CCSS.ELA-LITERACY.W.2.1, CCSS.ELA-LITERACY.W.2.5**)

In *The Jar of Happiness* by Ailsa Burrows, Meg thinks she has come up with a recipe for happiness that tastes like "apple juice and sunshine" and smells like "warm cookies and the ocean." She puts all her favorite things into the recipe and then whenever she comes across someone who is feeling glum, she shares some of her recipe with that person. Interestingly, despite it being a "recipe," people don't actually eat what's in the jar—Meg uses the jar to do things that make people happy, like making music or putting on a puppet show. Thus, she never runs out of the recipe, until the sad day when she looks for her jar and can't find it. Fortunately, the effort that Meg and her jar have put into cultivating happy friendships ensures that she will always have happiness as long as she has her friends.

Storytime (First Ten Minutes)

Invite the kids to have a seat on the floor while you read *The Jar of Happiness* by Ailsa Burrows. After reading, ask the kids to analyze the pictures and figure out how the Jar of Happiness actually works. Is it something Meg feeds to her friends, or is it something she uses to play with them?

Brainstorming (Next Ten Minutes) ··

Ask the kids to sit at the tables. Pass out the worksheet and ask the kids to write one thing that makes them happy in each box on the left side of the page. They can choose anything—a beloved toy, a favorite food, an activity they excel at, a funny book they've read, or a pretty place they've been.

Imagery and Figurative Language (Next Fifteen Minutes) ···············

Once they have ten things written down in the boxes, tell the kids to write in the column right next to each box one adjective that describes the way the word in the box would taste or smell. So if a kid has written "the beach" in one of his boxes, he will write how the beach smells or tastes—for example, "salty" or "hot." Push the child to imagine some magical ways one might manufacture the beach in a kitchen. Would it be stirred in a bowl of frothy waves, or baked in a sunshine oven?

What if a child wrote something like "playing the piano" in one of the boxes? Then she might want to use the next column to compare playing the piano to the taste or smell of something else. She might even have to think more imaginatively and use metaphorical or *figurative* language. I suggest doing at least a few examples like this together as a group. Explain to the kids that figurative language is language that is not meant to be taken literally. Figurative language will probably mean something slightly different to each person who hears it, and it will involve making a comparison of some kind.

So if a child wrote "playing the piano" as one of the things that make her happy, she could write about how else it makes her feel to play the piano. Does it make her feel accomplished? Proud? She can write that playing the piano "tastes like pride in myself." How would playing the piano smell? Maybe it would smell like a rich soup of melodies and rhythms. That phrase has no literal objective meaning, but when the child says it to herself, she can think about it and supply a meaning of her own.

The food and beverage industry already uses a lot of figurative language for describing taste and smell, many examples of which are borrowed from things that aren't even food-related in origin. Wine drinkers may describe a wine as having "notes" of black cherry, as though the wine were music and the notes were cherries. Then they might talk about the wine having a "hint" of vanilla, as though the vanilla is a secret scrawled on a piece of paper and handed to you with a wink. It's all just creative use of language. Share this example so that the kids are encouraged to get creative and poetic with their taste and smell ideas.

After the kids are done writing what each boxed item tastes or smells like, literally or figuratively, they are ready to cut the boxes into separate strips and put those strips into their jars.

Writing Labels (Next Twenty Minutes) ·····································

Now pass out the labels and ask the kids to write a poetic description for their happiness jars, based on the ingredients they have put in the jars and the way those ingredients taste and smell. They need to compile all those tastes and smells into only one or two sentences. This will be a challenge, because there is very little space to convey a lot of different concepts. It will take creativity, and perhaps even grouping or pairing of tastes, in order to get the description down to only one sentence.

If you have English language learners, give them a copy of the taste vocabulary sheet to help them find the words they may be looking for.

Decorating Labels (Last Ten Minutes) ··································

Allow the kids this time to decorate their labels and jars with stickers, glitter glue, foam shapes, and any other art supplies you might have available for them to use. Then finish by reminding the kids that, the next time they are feeling sad or low, or just out of ideas for writing, they can dip into their jars of happiness and enjoy an immediate rush of pleasant thoughts and memories.

NOTES

1. National Commission on Writing, *The Neglected "R": The Need for a Writing Revolution* (New York: College Board, 2003), 10–11.
2. Steve Graham and Dolores Perin, *Writing Next: Effective Strategies to Improve Writing of Adolescents in Middle and High Schools—A Report to Carnegie Corporation of New York* (Washington, DC: Alliance for Excellent Education, 2007), 7.
3. National Council of Teachers of English, "Professional Knowledge for the Teaching of Writing," www.ncte.org/positions/statements/teaching-writing.
4. Holly Lane and Stephanie Allen, "The Vocabulary-Rich Classroom: Modeling Sophisticated Word Use to Promote Word Consciousness and Vocabulary Growth," *Reading Teacher* 63, no. 5 (2010): 362–70.
5. Steven Ungerleider, "Visions of Victory," *Psychology Today*, last reviewed June 9, 2016, https://www.psychologytoday.com/articles/199207/visions-victory.

Write ten things that make you happy.	Write an adjective about its smell or taste (for example, *spicy, sweet, warm, sour*).	Compare it to something else: "It tastes like . . ." "It smells like . . ."
	....	....
	....	....
	....	....
	....	....
	....	....
	....	....
	....	....
	....	....
	....	....
	....	....

WORDS TO MAKE YOUR RECIPES SOUND YUMMY!

Delicious	Zesty
Tasty	Juicy
Crunchy	Tender
Scrumptious	Rich
Mouthwatering	Fresh
Succulent	Hearty
Luscious	Lip-smacking
Salty	Aromatic
Bitter	Creamy
Sweet	Delectable
Chewy	Flavorful
Syrupy	Moist
Spicy	Savory
Robust	Sizzling
Steamy	Sour
Tangy	

CHAPTER EIGHT

Books to Feed the Young Author's Spirit

One morning I was asking my first-grade daughter, who was sharing with me her latest writing project, whether she might want to be a writer when she grows up. Her eyebrows furrowed. "I *am* a writer," she said. "My teacher says so. She says it every day in Writer's Workshop." With a new glow of appreciation for the teacher my daughter was so fortunate to have, I said, "How silly of me! Of course you're a writer. So what's your next book going to be?"

It dawned on me that my daughter hasn't yet been infected by the Impostor Syndrome that grownups like me have struggled with for so long that we assume we were born with it. *We weren't* born with it—and we should take extra care not to infect our children and students with it. It's a dangerous illness that threatens to distance us from what Lucy McCormick Calkins and so many others have hailed as the "essential" philosophy in teaching young writers: that children be encouraged to "perceive themselves as authors."[1]

Children don't see any fundamental difference between who they are and who they want to be. They know they are not grownups with decades of experience behind them, but that doesn't concern them. Kids know, at some deep level, that they have limitless potential: all they have to do is try everything and practice often, and they will soon see what sticks.

But are we as adults prepared to treat them with the same confidence in their limitless potential? In their book *Already Ready: Nurturing Writers in Preschool and Kindergarten*, Matt Glover and Katie Wood Ray challenge teachers to see children as "the same kind of person as the most proficient writer, the same kind of person as Eric Carle, just with less experience."[2] When we make that mental leap of seeing our students not as children playing at being writers but as real writers-in-training, we are truly able to teach "the writer, not the writing."[3]

Librarians may be uniquely capable of making children feel like authors simply by showing them how the library nurtures writing. Writers belong in libraries as much as a pitcher belongs on a baseball field. Where else can you surround yourself with books and resources for research? And whether writers build libraries in their homes or seek out the libraries in public buildings, all great writers, without exception, are *readers*. So while we instill in children the sense that they *already* are writers, let's remind them often that reading is part of the daily routine of a writer and, therefore, something they should be doing all the time.

Billy's Booger: A Memoir (sorta) by William Joyce

In this picture book "memoir," William Joyce introduces us to "his younger self," a child whose funny and creative ideas aren't always appreciated at school. There, sports you invent yourself and illustrations on your math homework only earn you a reputation for being "odd" and "challenging." But when Billy hears about a book writing contest, he sees an opportunity to showcase his creativity in a more acceptable way. He works very hard on his entry, "Billy's Booger," which is included as a book-within-the-book. It is a humorous and imaginative book about a superhero booger who is sneezed out to save the world. Unfortunately, it does not meet the principal's criteria for things like "spelling" and "neatness." Using a rubric that emphasizes those aspects too strongly, other winners are chosen. But to Billy's surprise, the school librarian has entered all the books into the library's collection—even Billy's. And she tells him that his book is the most popular. Now Billy has a new motivation for imagining and creating, supported by friends who love his sense of humor.

You could use this book to announce a book writing contest at your library, and you could ask the kids in your workshop to come up with a better rubric for the judging. Then, like the librarian in the book, perhaps you could add the entries to the library's collection, or at least set aside a special shelf to showcase them. You can also fill that shelf with all the other books that kids have made from these writing programs!

I Am a Story by Dan Yaccarino

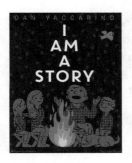

In *I Am a Story* by Dan Yaccarino, the essence of story-telling itself tells its own autobiography, from its beginnings at campfires and on cave walls, through the inventions of paper, wood blocks, tapestries, and printing presses, all the way to the modern mobile devices that enable people to download any story they want and take it wherever they wish to go. Story tells us how it has made people laugh and cry while shaping our culture in theater, radio, and TV. It shows us the different ways it has been shared in libraries and how it has survived despite being censored and burned. The final pages bring us back to Story's original campfire, reminding us that Story "will live forever."

Use this book to inspire kids to act out a fairy tale or write a fanfiction about their favorite movie characters. Talk about the many forms a story can take, and challenge kids to translate a story from one form to another.

Violet and Victor Write the Best-Ever Bookworm Book by Alice Kuipers, illustrated by Bethanie Deeney Murguia

Violet is a smart, confident (and sometimes bossy) young writer who enlists her twin brother Victor's help in writing a book. All she needs is a good story idea; so far, her main character (also called Violet) hasn't encountered any interesting problems. So Victor supplies a mystery for Violet to solve: someone is eating pages out of library books. Now Violet's protagonist has a goal—to track down the book-eating monster before it eats all the books in the library. Enter Victor's bookworm, who starts off as a spiky orange antagonist and, with a makeover from Violet, becomes a fuzzy, cute purple pet for her protagonist to tame. It's plain to see that Victor and Violet each have their own ideas about how the story should go. But despite their frequent clashes, they manage to create a book with lots of interesting alliteration and winning characters.

Use this book when you are planning a collaborative writing activity, to illustrate how collaboration can produce something great, as long as both writers feel they have ownership of it. You can also use the book to mentor kids on how to work together and how *not* to work together—to show the importance of respecting another person's ideas and not bossing that person around too much.

My Pen by Christopher Myers

This gorgeously drawn, black-and-white picture book explores the infinite number of things that can flow from an artist's pen. Even though the narrator is not rich or famous, he shows us how he can use his pen to take a ride on a dinosaur, sail to Africa, and tap dance on the sky! He can make giants of ordinary people and show the world how much he loves them. The book finishes with a suggestion to pick up a pen and unleash the "million worlds" hidden inside it! Kids will be mesmerized by the pictures and then immediately reach for a pen to write or draw.

The Sleeping Gypsy by Mordicai Gerstein

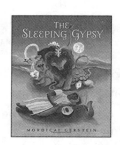

Mordicai Gerstein takes a mysterious and dreamlike painting by Henri Rousseau and invents a story about how the sleeping girl and the lion got there. He says that the girl in the desert originated in Rousseau's dreams. Tired from a long journey across the desert, the girl sits down beside a river, eats, and drinks. She sings a song while playing her mandolin and falls asleep on her blanket under the stars. That's when the animals come. It turns out there are more animals than just the lion we see in the painting! There's a lizard, a snake, a rabbit, a baboon, an ostrich, and a tortoise, all of whom have heard the girl's song and are wondering, like us, why she is here. When the lion jumps in and roars, "She is MINE!," he might be about to eat her—we don't know. But he is interrupted by a little man carrying a wooden case, who introduces himself as Henri Rousseau. Announcing that they are all in a dream, Rousseau begins to paint a group portrait. When he has finished, the animals critique the painting, complaining that he has made them "too fat," "too short," or "too ugly." Rousseau ignores their criticism and wipes them out of the painting altogether. But there is one animal whose demands he cannot ignore: the lion, who threatens to eat him if he does not paint the lion's mane beautifully. The next morning as the sun rises, we see that the lion kept quiet vigil over the girl, and the painter Henri Rousseau has awakened from his dream and is putting the finishing touches on his painting.

The artwork throughout is beautifully true to the original painting, and both the text and the illustrations bring the painting's story to life. Use this book to model great imagery and description, with such phrases as "a dome of darkening sky" and "bright worms of paint." You can also use this book to prompt your writers to tell stories about other famous works of art. I recommend reading an article by Denise Cassano on *Edutopia*: "Inspire Thoughtful Creative Writing through Art." Cassano provides tips for finding good artwork to use for creative writing. She suggests looking for images with these qualities:

- » Many details
- » Characters
- » Colors that shape a mood
- » Spatial relationships[4]

You could look for works of art housed at your local art museum, and after the workshop encourage the kids to visit the museum and see the real thing in person. You can even contact your nearest museum and see if the staff would be interested in some kind of partnership!

The Bear Report by Thyra Heder

Sophie is struggling to come up with ideas for her report on polar bears when suddenly a real polar bear appears in her living room. He introduces himself as Olafur and asks if Sophie would like to see where he lives. "No thanks," she says, "I've seen pictures." But Olafur takes her anyway to see his home "in person." Sophie is skeptical at first of the bare, ice-covered landscape, but Olafur shows her arctic foxes and snow rabbits hiding in burrows under the ice. He shows her that whales make music underwater and that the aurora borealis lights up the sky at night. Sophie learns the hard way how much farther apart the glaciers are getting from each other and how difficult this widening gap is for polar bears. But she uses her newfound whale language to hitch a ride back to shore. Sophie returns home full of enthusiasm for her project and uses maps, charts, and diagrams to teach her friends everything she has learned.

You can read this book to emphasize the importance of using interesting words and imagery, as Sophie goes from writing short, boring sentences to creating longer, more detailed sentences and diagrams. Whether kids are writing stories or reports, it's important that they learn to use sensory details, because reading about something ought to be the next best thing to seeing it "in person." Challenge the kids to take one page of the book painted in pretty watercolors and expand on it in writing, describing the scene so that we can see the sun shining on the ice and smell the cold, salty air.

The Best Story by Eileen Spinelli, illustrated by Anne Wilsdorf

Just like in *Billy's Booger*, our narrator is hard at work coming up with a story to win a writing contest at a library. The prize is pretty creative: a ride on a roller coaster with the author of a book about roller coasters! Because the author is her favorite, our narrator is eager to write the best story, and the members of her family are all eager to help. They have plenty of good ideas about writing—her brother says the story needs "action," her dad suggests "humor," her aunt says it should "make people cry," and her teenage sister says it needs to be "romantic." Unfortunately, writing a story that is all those things turns out to be a tall order. The narrator's story keeps changing because every time she gets somebody's input, she makes major adjustments. She hasn't yet learned to listen to her own feelings, but her heart is telling her something, because each time she makes a change to her story to please someone else, she feels that it is not "quite right." In the end, her mother advises her to listen to her heart, and she rewrites the story to be one that makes her happy. We don't get to find out whether the narrator wins the contest and the roller coaster ride or not. But she's written a story she is happy with and she knows now that that is more important.

Read this book to your students and discuss with them what kinds of revision are good and what kinds of revision might actually hurt a story. The struggles of the little girl in the book are struggles every writer has grappled with some point. Young writers are often used to conforming to whatever adults or authority figures tell them. Indeed, adults usually mean well and give good advice, as did everyone in this book. But kids have to learn that revising does not mean "making my book more pleasing to everybody." You can never please everybody. Revision requires you to have a vision for what your story will ideally be like so that when people give you feedback and advice, you only use the stuff that is going to help you get closer to that vision. How do you know that you're getting closer to your vision? Your heart and your gut will tell you; if it doesn't feel right, listen to that voice and think about it some more.

Inside This Book (Are Three Books)
by Barney Saltzberg

When my daughter was first learning to write letters, we wrote a book for her baby brother. She and I both drew pictures for it, and I helped her spell the names of the people and objects being depicted. We were inspired by this book by Barney Saltzberg, which shows how children of different ages and abilities approach the act of writing.

Three siblings of different ages are given blank books by their mother to draw or write whatever they wish. Their books are presented here, each one a little smaller than the one before it, and each one can be held up as a model for children to learn something about the writing life. Seymour is a thoughtful, reflective, and imaginative kid who fills his book with things he has seen and heard, his feelings, and his stories. He models for the reader how journaling and observing the world around you can make you a stronger writer. He includes one story for the reader: a comic strip about "A Funny Little Thing" that eats everything and becomes not-so-little. As Seymour's book ends, we see his sister Fiona's. Fiona is a poet who writes "a poem every day" and is proud of her ability to rhyme. She models self-confidence and the importance of taking daily time for writing. She shares her favorite poem about her dog, titled, "Who Wants to Play?" As her book ends, we see the youngest sibling Wilbur's book. He has drawn the pictures and his brother has helped him write the text. The book is very simple: "This is my family. This is a dinosaur. This is a dinosaur and my family!" What does Wilbur model? He models the fact that a person is never too young to be a writer—writing is not a practice reserved for people who know how to spell. The smallest child can write if she has someone to help her.

Use this book to inspire your students to help a younger sibling or friend put his ideas on paper. You can also do a collaborative book project in which you give one child a large blank book and another child a smaller blank book and then put the books together!

RECOMMENDED WEB RESOURCES

If my book has succeeded in its goal of inspiring you to give the "active" side of literacy a more active role in your library or your classroom, I hope that you now feel confident that you can take other children's books and come up with great writing programs inspired by them. Maybe you've even experienced the shift that I have felt in the way that I *read* children's books, ever since I first started doing writing workshops at the library. Just as writing changes the way that children read, teaching writing will change the way *you* read and will start to inform your ability to crystallize a book's qualities, which in turn will inform your readers' advisory practice and your collection development.

Now that you've undertaken this journey, allow me to point you in the direction of a few web resources that other librarians have created to help people find picture books that can teach creative writing concepts.

> » **Books to Support Readers' and Writers' Workshop** (*http://hs.mt laurelschools.org/subsites/Susan-Eley/documents/ReadWriteBooks.pdf*) Susan Eley, a school librarian in New Jersey, compiled this list of more than eight hundred children's books, organized by the aspect of creative writing that they can be used to teach (e.g., alliteration, adjectives). She makes the list available online through her school library's website.
> » **Teaching Skills with Children's Literature as Mentor Text** (*www.txla .org/sites/tla/files/conference/handouts/466teachteks.pdf*) Michelle Faught, Sheri McDonald, Sally Rasch, and Jessica Scheller presented this annotated bibliography of more than four hundred children's books, grouped by the creative writing concepts the books teach, at the Texas Library Association's annual conference in 2012. Their suggestions for children in the primary grades are preceded by a "Y" label for "younger students."
> » **Mentor Text Central!!** (*http://mentortextcentral.blogspot.com/*) Patty Young, a school librarian from California, writes this blog reviewing and labeling mentor texts for creative writing. You can click a link at the top of the home page to find all the blog posts she has written about books for "Grades PreK–2" as well as other categories.

CONCLUSION

In addition to using these great lists, I strongly recommend that you start keeping your own. A personal transformation comes from keeping your own list of children's books that inspire you. You will turn to it countless times for readers' advisory when you have parents or teachers looking for good picture books, and it will also become a fountain of ideas you can draw upon for creative writing programs.

Wherever you are in your journey to build literacy in the children you serve, I hope that you have as much fun doing these programs as the kids will have attending them!

NOTES

1. Lucy McCormick Calkins, *The Art of Teaching Writing* (Portsmouth, NH: Heinemann, 1986), 9.
2. Matt Glover and Katie Wood Ray, *Already Ready: Nurturing Writers in Preschool and Kindergarten* (Portsmouth, NH: Heinemann, 2008), 6.
3. Donald Graves, quoted in Allen Koshewa, "Finding the Heartbeat: Applying Donald Graves's Approaches and Theories," *Language Arts* 89, no. 1 (2011): 48.
4. Denise M. Cassano, "Inspire Thoughtful Creative Writing through Art," *Edutopia* (blog), August 7, 2014, https://www.edutopia.org/blog/thoughtful-creative-writing -through-art-denise-cassano.

When I first started doing these writing workshops, I bought lots of blank books for kids to write and draw pictures in, and I gave the books to the kids at each workshop so that they would have the added fun of making a "book" at the library!

But you don't actually have to buy blank books for your students. Blank books are easy to make. Many of the lessons in this book have a book template that you can download from our website: alaeditions.org/webextras.

Simply print the PDFs on 8½-by-11-inch paper in landscape orientation. The PDFs usually consist of one page that is both the front and the back cover, a second page that is numbered "page 1" on the right side and "page 4" on the left side, and a third page that is numbered "page 2" on the left side and "page 3" on the right side. After all three template pages have been printed, photocopy the "4 and 1" page and the "2 and 3" page to be on two sides of the same double-sided sheet of paper. You will typically need to feed one page into your copier's automatic feeder upside down in order for it to come out right.

Now you have two sheets of paper to work with: the sheet with your front and back covers and the sheet with all four of your internal pages.

Lay the cover page face down. Lay the other page on top of it, with numbers 2 and 3 shown face up. Then fold the sheets in half together, greeting card style, and staple them close to the folded edge. You will now have a book that has a front cover, four pages for writing and drawing, and a back cover on which kids will write an author bio.

Show the kids examples of author bios from your favorite picture books. In most humor picture books these days, the author writes something factual about himself, such as where he lives, and something witty about himself that has some relation to the story he is telling. Author bios do not have to be totally factual. If the child has written a book about a unicorn party full of balloons that pop, it would be relevant to readers to know whether the child knows many unicorns or what her favorite color balloon is.

Underneath the author bio, where it says "This book was published by: _____," you can put the name of your school or library and the city you are in. This notation will brand the book so that the child will always remember who encouraged him to write it!

SETUP

Who is in this story?

_____

What are they doing?

_____

Where is this happening?

_____

PROBLEM

What does each character want?

What happened?

Why did it happen?

How will this make each character feel?

RESOLUTION

How do the characters fix their problem?

_____

How do they feel once they have found a solution?

_____

How does this change the way they will act from now on?

_____

BIBLIOGRAPHY

Ackerman, Sara. "Becoming Writers in a Readers' World: Kindergarten Writing Journeys." *Language Arts* 93, no. 3 (2016): 200–12.

American Association of School Librarians. "Position Statement on the School Librarian's Role in Reading." Revised September 1, 2010. www.ala.org/aasl/advocacy/resources/statements/reading-role.

Anderson, Nancy L., and Connie Briggs. "Reciprocity between Reading and Writing: Strategic Processing as Common Ground." *Reading Teacher* 64, no. 7 (2011): 546–49.

Annie E. Casey Foundation. "Early Warning! Why Reading by the End of Third Grade Matters." 2010. www.aecf.org/resources/early-warning-why-reading-by-the-end-of-third-grade-matters/.

Bank Street Bookstore. "'If I Had a Raptor' and 'Olympians' with George O'Connor." YouTube video, 3:56. March 9, 2015. https://www.youtube.com/watch?v=7GgR3qACyZI.

Blumenfeld, Ally. "A Day in the Life of a Teen Writing Group." The Library as Incubator Project. www.libraryasincubatorproject.org/?p=18083.

Calkins, Lucy McCormick. *The Art of Teaching Writing.* Portsmouth, NH: Heinemann, 1986.

Cassano, Denise M. "Inspire Thoughtful Creative Writing through Art." *Edutopia* (blog), August 7, 2014. https://www.edutopia.org/blog/thoughtful-creative-writing-through-art-denise-cassano.

Common Core State Standards Initiative. "Key Shifts in English Language Arts." www.corestandards.org/other-resources/key-shifts-in-english-language-arts/.

Corden, Roy. "Developing Reading-Writing Connections: The Impact of Explicit Instruction of Literary Devices on the Quality of Children's Narrative Writing." *Journal of Research in Childhood Education* 21, no. 3 (2007): 269–89.

Cowan, Kay W. "Bridging the Theme: The Arts and Emergent Literacy." *Primary Voices K–6* 9, no. 4 (2001): 10–18.

Culham, Ruth. *The Writing Thief: Using Mentor Texts to Teach the Craft of Writing.* Newark, NJ: International Reading Association, 2014.

Freedman, Sarah Warshauer, et al. "Ten Years of Research: Achievements of the National Center for the Study of Writing and Literacy." Technical Report No. 1-C. National Writing Project (May 1995). https://www.nwp.org/cs/public/print/nwpr/587.

Fry, Edward Bernard, Jacqueline E. Kress, and Dona Lee Fountoukidis. *The ESL Teacher's Book of Lists,* 3rd ed. San Francisco: Jossey-Bass, 1993.

Fu, Danling, and Jane S. Townsend. "'Serious' Learning: Language Lost." *Language Arts* 76, no. 5 (1999): 404–11.

Gibson, Sharon A. "Effective Framework for Primary-Grade Guided Writing Instruction." Reading Rockets. www.readingrockets.org/article/effective-framework-primary -grade-guided-writing-instruction. Originally published in *Reading Teacher* 62, no. 4 (2008): 324–34.

Gillet, Jean Wallace, and Lynn Beverly. *Directing the Writing Workshop: An Elementary Teacher's Handbook.* New York: Guilford Press, 2001.

Glover, Matt, and Katie Wood Ray. *Already Ready: Nurturing Writers in Preschool and Kindergarten.* Portsmouth, NH: Heinemann, 2008.

Graham, Steve, and Dolores Perin. *Writing Next: Effective Strategies to Improve Writing of Adolescents in Middle and High Schools—A Report to Carnegie Corporation of New York.* Washington, DC: Alliance for Excellent Education, 2007.

Hinkle, Sarah. "Every Child Ready to Read: Best Practices." *Children and Libraries* (Fall 2014): 35–36.

James R. Squire Office of Policy Research. "Reading and Writing across the Curriculum: One Implication of CCSS; Research-Based Recommendations for Fostering RAWAC." National Council of Teachers of English (2011). www.theproecenter .info/uploads/2/2/5/5/22551316/reading_and_writing_across_the_curriculum .pdf.

Karambelas, Devin. "Study: Students Prefer Real Classrooms over Virtual." *USA Today,* June 11, 2013. www.usatoday.com/story/news/nation/2013/06/11/real -classrooms-better-than-virtual/2412401/.

Koshewa, Allen. "Finding the Heartbeat: Applying Donald Graves's Approaches and Theories." *Language Arts* 89, no. 1 (2011): 48–56.

Laliberty, Eloise Andrade, and Maria E. Berzins. "Creating Opportunities for Emerging Biliteracy." *Primary Voices K–6* 8, no. 4 (2000): 11–17.

Lane, Holly, and Stephanie Allen. "The Vocabulary-Rich Classroom: Modeling Sophis-ticated Word Use to Promote Word Consciousness and Vocabulary Growth." *Reading Teacher* 63, no. 5 (2010): 362–70.

Lukiv, Dan. "Home-Grown Publishing, Part Two: How to Develop a Creative Writing Program." CanTeach. www.canteach.ca/elementary/createwrite10.html.

Martin, Susan D., and Sherry Dismuke. "Common Core: Missing the Mark for Writing Standards." *Language Arts* 93, no. 4 (2016): 303.

Moffett, James. Introduction to *Collaboration through Writing and Reading,* edited by Anne H. Dyson, 21–24. Urbana, IL: National Council of Teachers of English, 1989.

National Commission on Writing. *The Neglected "R": The Need for a Writing Revolution.* New York: College Board, 2003.

National Council of Teachers of English. "Professional Knowledge for the Teaching of Writing." www.ncte.org/positions/statements/teaching-writing.

OCLC. "Perceptions of Libraries, 2010: Context and Community." https://www.oclc.org/ reports/2010perceptions.en.html.

Probus, Jessica. "This Video Will Show You How Dr. Seuss Actually Created His Books." BuzzFeed. January 10, 2015. https://www.buzzfeed.com/jessicaprobus/this -video-will-show-you-how-dr-seuss-created-his-books?utm_term=.fbx3 NegnG#.awkqRdyZ6.

Rowe, Deborah Wells, Joanne Deal Fitch, and Alyson Smith Bass. "Toy Stories as Opportunities for Imagination and Reflection in Writer's Workshop." *Language Arts* 80, no. 5 (2003): 363–74.

Ruiz, Nadeen T., Eleanor Vargas, and Angelica Beltran. "Becoming a Reader and Writer in a Bilingual Special Education Classroom." *Language Arts* 79, no. 4 (2002): 297–309.

Swaim, James F. "Laughing Together in Carnival: A Tale of Two Writers." *Language Arts* 79, no. 4 (2002): 337–47.

Tolentino, Efleda Preclaro. "'Put an Explanation Point to Make It Louder': Uncovering Emergent Writing Revelations through Talk." *Language Arts* 91, no. 1 (2013): 10–22.

Ungerleider, Steven. "Visions of Victory." *Psychology Today*. Last reviewed June 9, 2016. https://www.psychologytoday.com/articles/199207/visions-victory. Originally published in *Psychology Today* (July–August 1992): 46.

Wadham, Rachel L., and Terrell A. Young. *Integrating Children's Literature through the Common Core State Standards*. Santa Barbara, CA: Libraries Unlimited, 2015.

INDEX